ROMANS

A New Testament Commentary

Bob Yandian

Romans: A New Testament Commentary

ISBN : 978-168031-030-6
© 2015 by Bob Yandian
Bob Yandian Ministries
PO Box 55236
Tulsa, OK 74155
www.bobyandian.com

Published by Harrison House Publishers
Tulsa, OK 74155
www.harrisonhouse.com

18 17 16   10 9 8 7 6 5 4 3 2

Printed in the United States of America.

Table of Contents

ROMANS

VERSE BY VERSE COMMENTARY

The personal study notes of BOB YANDIAN

Introduction

My heart echoes a statement Peter made in His last epistle:

For this reason I will not be negligent to remind you always of these things, though you know and are established in the present truth.

2 Peter 1:12

The "for this reason" was to build on his previous statement — Peter's desire for all believers not just to get to heaven , but to have an abundant entrance into heaven. A working knowledge and practice of the word of God is necessary for an abundant entrance, which is marked by rewards and rulership.

In order to establish that abundant entrance, Peter taught believers what they should know again and again, repeatedly, "though you know them." What was taught them was the present truth. The present truth is what was being written in the day of the apostles Peter, Paul, John, and James.

This present truth is what believers still need to be gloriously saved. The Old Testament is to be studied in the light of the New Testament epistles. The four gospels are to be studied in the light of the New Testament epistles. Not only should every Christian know the epistles, they should be established in them.

This is why I have written this series of books, verse-by-verse teachings on the epistles of Paul, Peter, John and James. This is truly meat for our time period, our dispensation: the Church Age.

Bob Yandian
Author

Romans Overview

Writer: Paul the apostle, through the scribe Tertius (Romans 16:22).

Time: 58 AD, Romans 15:25, 26, (Compare to 1 Corinthians 16:1-3, 2 Corinthians 8:9).

Place of Writing: Corinth, from the house of Gaius (Romans 16:23).

Occasion: Phoebe is a businesswoman who has traveled from Corinth to Rome and delivers this letter.

Purpose

1. To clarify the principle of justification whether it is by deeds of the law or the work of God.

2. To explain the unbelief of Israel in the past, their failure in the previous dispensation, and how this can be remedied. This epistle expresses Paul's great concern for the Jewish people even though he is an apostle to the Gentiles.

3. To commend Phoebe to the Church at Rome (Romans 16:1).

4. To clarify the issue: What constitutes the Christian way of Life, Mosaic Law or New Law?

5. To help Roman believers understand how to have victory over the flesh.

Extremes of belief in Rome:

    a) No nature of the flesh after salvation

    b) Never any victory over the flesh so just sin until you die.

6. Protect Roman believers from the infiltration of legalism which had already made great inroads into Rome (Romans 13,14).

1:1–32 Paul and the Roman Believers

I. Opening Salutation (1–5)

1:1 ¶ Paul, a bondservant of Jesus Christ, called *to be* an apostle, separated to the gospel of God

Paul (means "little" in Greek), a servant (*doulos*: bondservant). A bondservant means someone else must do the providing. This is the importance of humility and also shows Paul has been purchased (1 Peter 1:18,19, Ephesians 1:7) of Jesus Christ, called to be (verb: Ephesians 1:4; past tense: Galatians 1:15) an apostle (see doctrine of apostleship, Galatians 1:1) separated (perfect tense) to the gospel of God.

1:2 which He promised before through His prophets in the Holy Scriptures,

Which (gospel of God) He promised before (aorist tense: OT scripture) through His prophets in the Holy Scriptures.

The gospel was clearly defined in the Old Testament so people were never saved by keeping the Mosaic Law or through animal sacrifices. Paul sets the record straight for the Roman believers in the opening of this epistle.

1:3-4 concerning His Son Jesus Christ our Lord, who was born of the seed of David according to the flesh, 4 *and* declared *to be* the Son of God with power according to the Spirit of holiness, by the resurrection from the dead.

The theme of Romans is the Lord Jesus Christ. Romans 1:3 teaches about His humanity. Verse 4 teaches of His Deity.

Concerning His Son, Jesus Christ (emphasizing humanity) our Lord who was born (came into being, John 1:14) of the seed of David (through Mary from Nathan Luke 3:23-31) according to (*kata*) the flesh.

And declared (aorist tense: mark out, define) to be the Son of God (deity) with power (omnipotence; this shows He could be man without losing any of His deity. Man and God can be united without sacrifice) according to (*kata*) the spirit of holiness (separation) (The Holy Spirit caused Jesus to become humanity—see Matthew 1:18-20.) by (from the source of) the resurrection from the dead.

1:5 Through Him we have received grace and apostleship for obedience to the faith among all nations for His name,

Through Christ, we have all received (aorist tense) grace and apostleship. Grace is received (Titus 2:11).

II. Recipients of the Epistle (6–7)

1:6 among whom you also are the called of Jesus Christ;

Among whom you also are called ("I was called—v. 1, and so are you—v. 6." This shows no favoritism in God's plan for each one of us) of Jesus Christ.

1:7 ¶ To all who are in Rome, beloved of God, called *to be* saints: ¶ Grace to you and peace from God our Father and the Lord Jesus Christ.

To all who are in Rome (believers) beloved (accepted: Ephesians 1:6, John 3:1, 2) of God, called to be saints (set apart ones).

Each spiritual gifts is a calling (v. 1, v. 6) and the fact that we are saints is a calling (v. 7). This all goes back to foreknowledge, the basis for predestination (Romans 8:29).

...grace to you and peace.

Grace always precedes peace. Grace is the foundation for peace. Without a knowledge of grace, there can be no foundation for peace.

...from God our Father and the Lord Jesus Christ.

Both grace and peace are gifts from our Father to us through the mediator Jesus Christ.

III. Paul's Attitude Toward the Roman Believers (8–10)

1:8 ⁋ First, I thank my God through Jesus Christ for you all, that your faith is spoken of throughout the whole world.

First, I thank (keep on thanking) my God, through Jesus Christ for you all (All praise to the Father goes through the mediator.), that your faith (use of faith) is spoken of (constantly spoken of) throughout the whole (Roman) world.

1:9 For God is my witness, whom I serve with my spirit in the gospel of his Son, that without ceasing I make mention of you always in my prayers;

All motivation for Paul' life came from his spirit. He would not be dictated to by his soul. He dictated to his soul. He pulled every thought into captivity just like he kept his body under.

...in the gospel of His Son (Paul was strong in the word) that without ceasing I make mention of you always in my prayers (Paul was also strong in prayers. He prayed for the Roman believers by name—see 16:1-16).

1:10 making request if, by some means, now at last I may find a way in the will of God to come to you.

The purpose of Paul's prayer for some time was to have a prosperous journey to come to the Romans.

IV. Three Purposes of Paul's Visit (11–13)

1:11 For I long to see you, that I may impart to you some spiritual gift, so that you may be established—

The first purpose was to give stability to the believers by the teaching of the word .

For I long (desire intensely) to see you, that I may impart (share something of importance) to you some spiritual gift.

Paul wants to share from his spiritual gifts with the Roman believers and even to impart to others (The Lord through Paul), a spiritual gift.

...so that you may be established (passive voice: receive stability).

1:12 that is, that I may be encouraged together with you by the mutual faith both of you and me.

That is, that I may be comforted together with you by the mutual faith both of you and me.

The second purpose was to provide comfort.

That is (for this purpose) that I may be encouraged together with you (share a mutual blessing) by the mutual faith both of you and me.

The measure of faith possessed by both Paul and the Roman saints will be increased and cause joint blessing.

1:13 ¶ Now I do not want you to be unaware, brethren, that I often planned to come to you (but was hindered until now), that I might have some fruit among you also, just as among the other Gentiles.

The third purpose was to see production by the Roman believers.

Now I do not want (do not desire) you to be unaware brothers that I often planned to come to you, but was hindered until now.

Paul was restrained by the Holy Spirit until now probably to allow the Roman church to get going on their own.

V. Paul's Three "I Ams" (14–17)

A. I Am a Debtor

1:14 I am a debtor both to Greeks and to barbarians, both to wise and to unwise.

I am a debtor (of the gospel) both to the Greeks and to the barbarians;

All our debts were paid on the cross and we owe God nothing. But the debt to the world has not been paid. Jesus began to pay this debt when He preached the gospel, but never paid it off. He has passed that debt on to us through the Great Commission. We continue to pay the debt to the world by preaching the gospel to them, then hand it on to the next generation after us. It is to be preached to all. The first mentioned is to the educated and uneducated.

...both to wise and unwise (amplification of Greeks and barbarians).

B. I Am Ready

1:15 So, as much as is in me, I am ready to preach the gospel to you who are in Rome also.

You can only give out of what you know.

C. I Am Not Ashamed

1:16 ¶ For I am not ashamed of the gospel of Christ, for it is the power of God to salvation for everyone who believes, for the Jew first and also for the Greek.

For I am not ashamed of the gospel (which is) of Christ, for it is the power (*dunamis*) of God to salvation for everyone who believes (present active)...

God's power for salvation is only toward those who believe (Ephesians 1:19, Isaiah 53:1).

...for the Jew first (Old Testament) and also for the Greek (New Testament).

1:17 For in it the righteousness of God is revealed from faith to faith; as it is written, "The just shall live by faith."

For in it (in the gospel) the righteousness of God is revealed.

Only through the preaching of the gospel, found in the word of God, is God's righteousness revealed. The arm of the Lord (salvation, righteousness) is revealed to those who believe the report (Isaiah 53:1).

...from faith (point of salvation, see Romans 3:28) to faith (daily operational faith, after salvation, see Hebrews 11:6, 2 Corinthians 5:7) as it is written (Habakkuk 2:4) the just (those already saved) shall live by Faith.

This introduces one part of the purpose of this book. You are not saved by legalism and are not spiritual by legalism either. You are saved by faith and are spiritual by faith (Galatians 3:17).

VI. God Consciousness (18–32)

1:18 ¶ For the wrath of God is revealed from heaven against

all ungodliness and unrighteousness of men, who suppress the truth in unrighteousness,

For the wrath of God is revealed from heaven (toward those who reject the gospel at God consciousness) against all ungodliness (heathenism, idolatry—subject of chapter 1) and the unrighteousness of men (moral and religious people who stand on their own righteousness —Isaiah 64:6. This will be the subject of chapter 2) who suppress (hold down) the truth in unrighteousness.

God consciousness is the point where each person realizes there is a God. This does not bring salvation, but does open the door for the gospel to be presented. When a person reaches God consciousness, God has an obligation to send someone to give the gospel, no matter where the person lives or the environment or culture he or she lives in.

A. The Point of God Consciousness

1:19 because what may be known of God is manifest in them, for God has shown *it* to them.

Because what (reason for God's wrath) may be known of (about, concerning) God is manifest (made plain) in (inside) them, for God has shown it to them.

1:20 For since the creation of the world His invisible *attributes* are clearly seen, being understood by the things that are made, *even* His eternal power and Godhead, so that they are without excuse,

This verse shows how God has shown Himself to them.

For since the creation of the world,(*kosmos*: world's system) His invisible attributes are clearly seen (perceived rationally) being understood by the things that are made (nature) even (namely) His eternal power and Godhead, so that they (heathen who reject the gospel) are without excuse.

1:21 because, although they knew God, they did not glorify *Him* as God, nor were thankful, but became futile in their thoughts, and their foolish hearts were darkened.

Because although (they are without excuse for this reason) they knew God (*ginosko*: knew about God) they did not glorify Him as God, nor were thankful, but became futile (empty) in their thoughts (reasonings) and their foolish hearts were darkened (passive voice: received darkness).

What light had penetrated their heart by the hearing of the gospel was removed at their rejection of the gospel. This was done by their own free will (passive voice). They opened up and received darkness into their heart toward God's message of eternal life.

1:22 Professing themselves to be wise, they became fools,

Professing to be wise, they became fools (passive voice: received foolishness).

1:23 and changed the glory of the incorruptible God into an image made like corruptible man—and birds and four-footed animals and creeping things.

They began to worship what they could see instead of what they could not see, the true God.

B. The Result of Rejecting God Consciousness

1:24 ¶ Therefore God also gave them up to uncleanness, in the lusts of their hearts, to dishonor their bodies among themselves,

Therefore God also gave them up (handed them over)

They gave up God, and God gave them up also. God did to them what they had done to Him (scorns the scorner—the one scorning Him—Proverbs 3:34).

...to uncleanness (sexual impurity, no fixed standard) in the (by means of) lusts of their hearts to dishonor (abuse, degrade) their bodies among themselves.

1:25 who exchanged the truth of God for the lie, and worshipped and served the creature rather than the Creator, who is blessed forever. Amen.

Who exchanged the truth of God for the lie, and worshipped and served (religious service) the creature (creation) rather than the Creator, who is blessed forever. Amen.

1:26 ¶ For this reason God gave them up to vile passions. For even their women exchanged the natural use for what is against nature.

For this reason God gave them up to vile passions. For even their women exchanged the natural use (men with women) for what is against (contrary to) nature.

For women to change the natural use, shows that lesbianism is a choice, not a result of natural birth. It also shows lesbianism is unnatural, against nature.

1:27 Likewise also the men, leaving the natural use of the woman, burned in their lust for one another, men with men committing what is shameful, and receiving in themselves the penalty of their error which was due.

Likewise also, the men, leaving the natural use of the woman (normal sexual relations).

Just like the woman, for men to leave the natural use of the woman shows a choice, not a result of natural birth.

...burned (sexually inflamed) in their lusts for one another (*allos*), men with men committing what is shameful (indecent) and receiving in themselves the penalty (retribution) of their error which was due (inevitable).

Lust is consistently used for homosexuality and lesbianism (vv.24-27). Lust is not a sickness, but a sin. Homosexuality and lesbianism are sin. Sodom and Gomorrah and three other cities were all destroyed because of homosexuality and lesbianism. Today that area is the Dead Sea.

1:28 ¶ And even as they did not like to retain God in their knowledge, God gave them over to a debased mind, to do those things which are not fitting;

And even as (just like) they did not like to retain God in their knowledge,

God gave (delivered) them over to a debased mind, to do those things which are not fitting (proper, normal).

C. The Effects of Rejecting God Consciousness

1:29 being filled with all unrighteousness, sexual immorality, wickedness, covetousness, maliciousness; full of envy, murder, strife, deceit, evil-mindedness; *they are* **whisperers,**

Being filled (*pleroma*: completely filled) with all unrighteousness. The next sins are used to describe unrighteousness:

1. Sexual immorality: illicit sex between a man and woman

2. Wickedness: outward displays of evil

3. Covetousness: lust toward the pleasures and possessions of life

4. Maliciousness: inner mental evil

5. Seven Attitudes of Evil

   a) Full of envy: mental attitude of jealously

   b) Murder: taking of innocent life

   c) Strife: bickering

   d) Deceit: fraud, treachery, lack of loyalty

   e) Evil mindedness: tendency to find fault with anything you do not originate or suggest.

   f) Whisperers: private gossiper, secret slanderer

   g) Backbiters: open gossiper, slanderer

1:30 backbiters, haters of God, violent, proud, boasters, inventors of evil things, disobedient to parents,

D. Attitudes Toward God and His Institutions

1. Haters of God: antagonistic toward God and anything from Him.

2. Violent: insolent

3. Proud: ego (original sin of Lucifer - Isaiah 14:14).

4. Boasters: overt expression of pride

5. Inventors of evil things: creating new forms of evil (wicked imaginations)

6. Disobedient to parents: undisciplined children

1:31 undiscerning, untrustworthy, unloving, unforgiving, unmerciful;

1. Undiscerning: no comprehension of God's natural and divine laws.

2. Untrustworthy: people who cannot keep their word.

3. Unloving: no mercy or compassion for others. No reconciliation unless the others totally submit to him.

4. Unforgiving: no compassion for the mistakes of others.

5. Unmerciful: distortion of life and love attitudes.

Homosexuality and lesbianism are not the only signs of heathenism, but any of the things mentioned in verses 29-31. You cannot look for heathenism and just look for one sin. It goes deeper and in many directions.

1:32 who, knowing the righteous judgment of God, that those who practice such things are deserving of death, not only do the same but also approve of those who practice them.

Who knowing the righteous judgment of God (Heathenism knows one area of the word , God's judgment) that those who practice (*poieo*: habitually practice) such things are deserving of death, not only do the same, but also approve those who practice them.

2:1–29 Self-Righteous and Religious Man

The first half of this chapter deals with the self-righteous, unbelieving man. The second half deals with the religious man whether unbeliever or believer.

I. The Self-Righteous Man (1–11)

2:1 ¶ Therefore you are inexcusable, O man, whoever you are who judge, for in whatever you judge another you condemn yourself; for you who judge practice the same things.

Therefore (because of those things in chapter 1) you are inexcusable, oh man...

This man is a self-righteous unbeliever who does not commit (outwardly) the sins of adultery, murder, theft, etc. He looks down his nose at others who do. He is just as guilty. He thinks he will get to heaven because he has done so many good deeds and refrained from evil deeds.

...whoever you are that judges: for in whatever you judge another (*heteros*: another of a different kind), you condemn yourself: for you that judges does (practice) the same thing.

The self-righteous man may not sin outwardly, but does so inwardly. He judges others who do sin outwardly, but are guilty also of inward sins of the heart, thoughts. When he judges others who do not live up to his standard, this is inward, mental sin.

2:2 But we know that the judgment of God is according to truth against those who practice such things.

But we know that the judgment of God (Great White Throne) is according to (*kata*: the standard of) truth (the gospel, the word of God) against those (immoral, moral, religious) who commit (practice) such things.

2:3 And do you think this, O man, you who judge those practicing such things, and doing the same, that you will escape

the judgment of God?

And do you think (rationalize), oh man, who judges those who do (practice) such things, and do the same, that you will escape the judgment of God?

These people think God will grade on a curve and they will rate high. God's standard is 100% before you can pass. Anything less and you fail. One hundred percent is God's righteousness. One man has passed, Jesus Christ. If you do not depend on your own good works, but depend on the finished work of Jesus on the cross, you will be given His grade. He has taken the test and passed. It is not cheating for Him to give you His 100% in exchange for you failing grade.

2:4 Or do you despise the riches of His goodness, forbearance, and longsuffering, not knowing that the goodness of God leads you to repentance?

The self-righteous man does not understand grace.

Or do you despise the riches of His goodness and forbearance and longsuffering? not knowing that the goodness of God leads you to repentance (*metanoeo*: changing of the mind).

The problem with the self-righteous man is he believes God thinks like he does. The self-righteous man does not understand God's longsuffering, patience and grace. He wonders why God does not immediately punish all those in obvious sin. So he goes about to help God by maligning and gossiping. Yet if he ever slips, he wants grace and long-suffering from God.

2:5 But in accordance with your hardness and your impenitent heart you are treasuring up for yourself wrath in the day of wrath and revelation of the righteous judgment of God,

But after (in accordance with) your hardness (*skleruno*: callous) and impenitent (unchanging) heart you are treasuring up for yourself wrath in the day of wrath (White Throne— see Revelation 20) and revelation of the righteous judgment of God;

2:6 who "will render to each one according to his deeds":

Who (God) will render (refund, pay back) to every man (unbeliever) according to his deeds (good deeds).

A. Eternal Punishment
Verses 2 and 6 tell the two things that will send a person to eternal punishment.

1. In verse 2, "according to the truth", the gospel which teaches faith in Jesus Christ as the only means of eternal life.

2. In verse 6, "according to his deeds", good deeds. Since the unbeliever has rejected the righteousness of Jesus, he falls back on his own good deeds, his righteousness.

   a) At the Great White Throne Judgment, the unbeliever will stand before God in a resurrection body and stand on his own good deeds since he has rejected the works of Jesus. He will stand on his own grade, not Jesus'.

   b) He will not be judged for his sins because Jesus died for them. Sins will never be held against anyone for entrance into heaven and eternity with God.

   c) Revelation 20:12-15 says the dead (spiritually) are judged from two books, The Book of Works (good deeds) and The Book of Life (Lamb's Book of those who have accepted Jesus).

   d) Unbelievers are judged first from the Book of Works. They may stand on their good deeds, but will be shown by God to have received a failing grade. Their human righteousness will never equal God's righteousness.

   e) Unbelievers are finally judged from the Book of Life and sentenced to the lake of fire because their name was there at one time, but later blotted out and not found when they died after rejecting Jesus in their lifetime (Revelation 20:15).

B. Believer Who Accepts
Verse(s) 7 (and 10) teach of the believer who accepts the work of the cross.

2:7 eternal life to those who by patient continuance in doing good seek for glory, honor, and immortality;

To them who by patient continuance in well doing (persevering in the daily Christian walk) seek for glory and honor (rewards), and immortality, eternal life:

The book of works will be used for eternal blessing and rewards for the believer, if those works were done in the energy of the Spirit, and in fellowship with God.

C. Unbeliever Who Rejects
Verses 8 and 9 teach of the unbeliever who rejects the work of the cross and accepts his own works.

2:8 but to those who are self-seeking and do not obey the truth, but obey unrighteousness—indignation and wrath,

But unto them who are contentious (self-seeking) and do not obey the truth (believe on Jesus Christ), but obey unrighteousness (human works), indignation and wrath,

Four things come to those who obey unrighteousness: indignation, wrath, tribulation and anguish.

2:9 tribulation and anguish, on every soul of man who does evil, of the Jew first and also of the Greek;

Tribulation and anguish on every soul of man that does (works out) evil (good deeds of man) to the Jew first (the Jew received the gospel first, in the Old Testament and from Jesus also) and also to the Greek (Church Age).

2:10 but glory, honor, and peace to everyone who works what is good, to the Jew first and also to the Greek.

But (contrast) glory, honor and peace to every man who works good (Greek-the good) to the Jew first, and also to the Greek.

The good which is worked out is first acceptance of Jesus according to the scriptures, then the working out of good works under the power of the Holy Spirit in life as a witness to the unbeliever.

2:11 For there is no partiality with God.

For there is no respect (partiality) with God (Ephesians 6:9, Colossians 3:25, James 2:1-10).

II. The Religious Man (12–29)

A. Guilty of Transgressing Law

2:12 ¶ For as many as have sinned without law will also perish without law, and as many as have sinned in the law will be judged by the law

For as many as have sinned (rejected Jesus) without (outside) law (heathen) shall also perish without (outside) law.

The moral or religious man is just as guilty as the immoral and heathen man. and as many as have sinned in the law will be judged by the law (this sentence will be completed in verse 16). This is the law for the Jew and Gentile. The Mosaic Law for the Jew and self-righteousness for the Gentile. Verses 13-15 are a parenthetical amplification of the principle in verse 12.

2:13 (for not the hearers of the law are just in the sight of God, but the doers of the law will be justified;

For not the hearers (learners) of the law who are just before (in the sight of God), but (this is an assumption) the doers (performers, the ones who practice) the law will (someday) be justified.

The assumption by the religious person is that not just knowing the law is important, but doing it will bring salvation. This is salvation by works which Paul will now refute.

2:14 for when Gentiles, who do not have the law, by nature do the things in the law, these, although not having the law, are a law to themselves,

For when Gentiles who do not have the law by nature (instinct) do the things in the law, these although not having the law, are a law to themselves.

Paul refutes the religious Jews who think they are righteous and perfect before God because they not only know and memorize the law, they obey it. But the Gentiles, the heathen, keep the law by instinct, knowing through intuition the existence of right and wrong, good and evil. Without a law, they know certain things are wrong which the Jews pride themselves in obeying (murder, adultery, stealing, lying, etc.).

2:15 who show the work of the law written in their hearts, their conscience also bearing witness, and between themselves *their* thoughts accusing or else excusing *them*)

There are certain qualities of life that every person possesses in his heart which also his mind bears witness to. "I don't know why this is wrong, I just know it is," and their thoughts (thinking) accuse or else excuse them. The Gentiles judge each other by an instinctive law in their hearts and minds and produce a righteousness which is just as good as that produced by the Jews who have the law. But it is all self-righteousness. The argument is this: If the Gentiles can produce the same righteousness without the law, and not be saved, then there is no reason to have the law for salvation.

The same is true for spirituality. If quitting sin—lying, stealing, getting drunk—makes you spiritual, why have faith in Jesus? The unbeliever can do the same.

2:16 in the day when God will judge the secrets of men by Jesus Christ, according to my gospel.

In the day when God (Great White Throne) will judge the secrets (hidden things) of men by Jesus Christ according to (the standard of) my gospel.

All unbelievers (heathen, moral, and religious) will be judged according to the gospel.

B. Religious Man's Boasting

2:17 ¶ Indeed you are called a Jew, and rest on the law, and make your boast in God,

Behold, you are called a Jew and rest in (rely, depend on) the law (for salvation) and make your boast in God (know God intimately)

2:18 and know *His* will, and approve the things that are excellent, being instructed out of the law,

And know (claim to know) His will, and approve (test) the things (of life) that are more excellent, being instructed out of the law;

The Jew in his superior thinking not only believes he knows the law, but is the teacher to others of right and wrong, spirituality and carnality.

2:19 and are confident that you yourself are a guide to the blind, a light to those who are in darkness,

And are confident that you yourself are a guide to the blind (unbeliever) a (supposed) light to those who are in darkness (unbelief).

The religious Jew is exactly who Jesus was referring to when he called them, "the blind (religious) leading the blind (heathen)."

2:20 an instructor of the foolish, a teacher of babes, having the form of knowledge and truth in the law.

An instructor of the foolish (Gentiles, heathen) a teacher of babies, having the form (framework) of the knowledge and truth in the law.

The Jews are worse than the Gentiles because they actually have the framework of true knowledge and God's truth, but they worship the frame and not the picture. The law teaches we are a sinner, then points us to the Author of salvation, the answer to our sin, Jesus Christ. The Jews worshipped the law and not Who and what it taught: salvation through Jesus Christ.

C. Religion Not Righteousness

2:21 You, therefore, who teach another, do you not teach yourself? You who preach that a man should not steal, do you steal?

You (Jew) therefore who teach another, do you not teach yourself? You who preach that a man should not steal (commandment number eight), do you steal?

Jesus preached about the stealing the Jews did of the widows (Matthew 23:14). They took money from those who could least afford it.

2:22 You who say, "Do not commit adultery," do you commit adultery? You who abhor idols, do you rob temples?

You who say, do not commit adultery (commandment number seven), do you commit adultery?

Jesus qualified adultery as not only the act, but the lust in the heart (Matthew 5:27-28). It was also reported in Jesus' day that the Pharisees were well known among the prostitutes. The Jewish religious leaders were quick to participate in the things they preached against.

You who abhor idols (commandment number one), do you commit sacrilege (rob temples)?

For many years, the Pharisees and religious Jews robbed Gentile temples of gold and silver and kept it for themselves, claiming it belonged to God and His work.

2:23 You who make your boast in the law, do you dishonor God through breaking the law?

"Do you dishonor God by breaking the law? YES."

2:24 For "the name of God is blasphemed among the Gentiles because of you," as it is written.

The name of Jehovah was so revered among the Jews that they would not speak it. But by their actions, they caused the Gentiles to blaspheme that sacred name.

2:25 ¶ For circumcision is indeed profitable if you keep the law; but if you are a breaker of the law, your circumcision has become uncircumcision.

For circumcision is indeed profitable, if you keep (observe) the law: but if you break (are a transgressor) of the law your circumcision (physical) has become uncircumcision.

This will be amplified later. The law was given to the unbeliever to learn of Christ who gives righteousness. Then it can be fulfilled by the one who has been made righteous. Only a righteous person can fulfill the law.

2:26 Therefore, if an uncircumcised man keeps the righteous requirements of the law, will not his uncircumcision be counted as circumcision?

Therefore, if an uncircumcised man (Gentile) keeps (fulfills) the righteous requirements of the law (by accepting Jesus as savior), will not his uncircumcision (physical) be counted as circumcision (spiritual)?

Titus was a Gentile who was uncircumcised. Yet Paul used him to prove salvation comes to those who believe, not to those who have kept the commandments of the law (Galatians 2:1-3). Paul is simply asking the question, "Which is more important, the sign or the reality?" Just as circumcision was given as a sign of salvation, $ is a symbol for money, but it is not money.

2:27 And will not the physically uncircumcised, if he fulfills the law, judge you who, *even* with *your* written *code* and circumcision, *are* a transgressor of the law?

And will not uncircumcision (the physically uncircumcised or Gentiles) if he fulfils the law (accepts Jesus), judge you, who by the letter and circumcision (who even with your written code of the Mosaic Law) and circumcision are a transgressor of the law?

2:28 For he is not a Jew who *is* one outwardly, nor *is* circumcision that which *is* outward in the flesh;

For he is not a Jew, which is one outwardly (a descendant of Abraham, Isaac, and Jacob), neither is that circumcision, which is outward in the flesh.

2:29 but *he is* a Jew who *is one* inwardly; and circumcision *is that* of the heart, in the Spirit, not in the letter; whose praise *is* not from men but from God.

But he is a Jew, which is one inwardly (Romans 9:6, "not all Israel is Israel) and circumcision is that of the heart (spiritual birth) in the spirit (amplification of "the heart") not in the letter (Law of Moses) whose praise is not from men, but from God.

True salvation gives glory to God and not the efforts of man.

3:1–31 The Law or Faith

I. Advantage of Judaism is the Law (1–4)

3:1 ¶ What advantage then has the Jew, or what *is* the profit of circumcision?

What advantage then has the Jew (racial), or what is the profit of circumcision (religious)?

Paul is saying, "If the law, being a Jew, or circumcision doesn't save, what advantage is there of being a physical or religious Jew."

3:2 Much in every way! Chiefly because to them were committed the oracles of God.

Much in every way: chiefly (many reasons, but mainly) because to them were committed the oracles of God.

The law was given only to the Jews. It remains for the instruction of Christians today, but as with the Jew, is not for salvation or spirituality.

3:3 For what if some did not believe? Will their unbelief make the faithfulness of God without effect?

For what if (and it is) some did not believe (and some did not)? Shall their unbelief make the faithfulness of God without effect (null and void)? No one's unbelief can change God's immutability.

3:4 Certainly not! Indeed, let God be true but every man a liar. As it is written: "That You may be justified in Your words, And may overcome when You are judged."

God forbid (certainly not or let it not be so, indeed) let God be true but every man a liar...

Even if every man was a liar, God would still be true. Man's opinion does not change God's understanding.

...As it is written, (Psalm 51:4) That You (God) might be justified (vindicated) in Your sayings (words) and might overcome when You (God) are judged.

God's yes is always yes and His no, no. He is vindicated by His own mouth, not man's.

II. Righteousness, Unrighteousness, and the Law (5–20)

A. Breaking Down Jewish Beliefs about Righteousness
In verse 5, Paul is using debater's technique. He is using an actual argument the Jewish leaders are giving and assuming they are right, to prove them wrong in their beliefs about righteousness.

> **3:5 ⸱ But if our unrighteousness demonstrates the righteousness of God, what shall we say?** *Is* **God unjust who inflicts wrath? (I speak as a man.)**

But if (let's assume) our unrighteousness commend (demonstrates, promotes) the righteousness of God, what (conclusion) shall we say (come to)? Is God unrighteous (unjust) who takes vengeance (inflicts wrath)? (I speak as a man [human viewpoint].)

In other words, if the more I sin, the more God is promoted and helped, How could He condemn me?
First, God needs no help. His righteousness is self-existent. This is all leading up to a point, How can a loving God cast His creatures into the lake of fire?
In review, If my unrighteousness promotes God's righteousness, then we can only come to one conclusion, God is unrighteous for His judgment! This is blasphemy! Since God is righteous, then our unrighteousness never promotes His righteousness.

> **3:6 Certainly not! For then how will God judge the world?**

God forbid (certainly not! May it never be) For then (if this be true) how shall God judge the world?

A judge must have a standard to judge by. God's standard is His righteousness. Remove His righteousness and He is not capable of judgment.

> **3:7 ⸱ For if the truth of God has increased through my lie to His glory, why am I also still judged as a sinner?**

For (let's assume this to be true) if the truth of God has more abounded (increased because of) my lie to His glory, why am I also still judged as a sinner?

Paul makes the assumption personal. If my lies promote God's righteousness, then I cannot be judged as a sinner. If lying promotes God, there is no such thing as sin, and finally no such thing as a sinner. All unrighteousness promotes God's righteousness. Unrighteousness loses its meaning and there is no unrighteousness. No unrighteousness means no sinners. No unrighteousness means no righteousness because there is no more standard to judge unrighteousness by. God then is not righteous.

3:8 And *why* not say, "Let us do evil that good may come"?—as we are slanderously reported and as some affirm that we say. Their condemnation is just.

And not rather (as we are slanderously reported, and as some affirm that we say,) Let us do evil, that good may come? whose damnation (condemnation, judgment) is just.

Some are saying Paul is preaching evil. The message of grace is evil. They are asking, "Does the end justify the means? Can grace bring salvation? Can evil bring good?" Paul says that the judgment is correct. Evil cannot produce good, but they, not he, are doing the evil by preaching salvation by works.
Now the Jews are getting upset because Paul is saying that Gentiles are as good as Jews.

3:9 ¶ What then? Are we better than they? Not at all. For we have previously charged both Jews and Greeks that they are all under sin.

What then? Are we (Jews) better than they (Gentiles)? No, in no way: for we have (aorist tense: once and for all) before proved (previously charged: Romans 1:18-32, 2:1-14,15-29) both Jews and Gentiles, that they are all under sin (the sin or flesh nature);

Paul has, up until now, stated the advantages of being Jew, but not their superiority. Sin singular refers to the flesh, the sin nature, the curse introduced on the earth and humanity at the fall.

B. God's Righteousness

All are judged sinners by an absolute standard, the righteousness of God, and Paul uses the Old Testament for the benefit of an indictment of the Jew.

3:10 ¶ As it is written:"There is none righteous, no, not one;

None righteous means moral, immoral, religious, non-religious, male, female, educated, uneducated, Jew or Gentile.

3:11 There is none who understands; There is none who seeks after God.

An unregenerate man has no understanding of God, or truly cares to search for God.

3:12 They have all turned aside; They have together become unprofitable; There is none who does good, no, not one."

They have all gone out of the way (turned aside from the way of salvation); They have together become unprofitable (depraved); There is none who does good (divine good), no, not one.

C. Man's Sin

3:13 "Their throat is an open tomb; With their tongues they have practiced deceit"; "The poison of asps is under their lips";

Open graves spew out smells of death, decaying bodies. **And out of the abundance of the heart, the mouth speaks** (Psalm 5:9).

...with their tongues they have used (practiced) deceit (false doctrine); the poison of asps (Egyptian cobra) is under their lips:

3:14 "Whose mouth *is* full of cursing and bitterness."

Whose mouth is full of cursing (toward God) and bitterness (toward man—see Psalm 10:7).

3:15 "Their feet *are* swift to shed blood;

Their feet are swift to shed blood (true of heathen and religious alike—Isaiah 59:7-8):

3:16 Destruction and misery *are* in their ways;

Destruction (torture) and misery (harassment) are in their ways:

They have not gone after the way of God (v. 12), but after their own ways (Isaiah 53:6).

3:17 And the way of peace they have not known. 18 There is no fear of God before their eyes."

There is no fear (reverence) of God before their eyes.

D. True Purpose of the Mosaic Law
It was given by God and must have a purpose (see Psalm 36:1)

3:19 ¶ Now we know that whatever the law says, it says to those who are under the law, that every mouth may be stopped, and all the world may become guilty before God.

Now (in view of what we have just studied, all are condemned) we know that whatever the law says, it says to those who are under the law (The ones under the law are unbelievers of all races—1Timothy 1:9, 10) that every mouth (Jew, Gentile, moral, immoral) may be stopped, and all the world may become guilty before God.

Stopping all mouths is the purpose of the law. By trying to keep the law, eventually your mouth is stopped and you find yourself guilty before God.

3:20 Therefore by the deeds of the law no flesh will be justified in His sight, for by the law *is* the knowledge of sin.

Therefore (the logical conclusion) by the deeds of the law no flesh will be justified in His sight (Great White Throne Judgment), for by the law is the knowledge of sin (sin nature, flesh).

By trying to keep the law you cannot be saved. You cannot keep the law by keeping the law. You keep the law by trust in Jesus as savior and afterwards, walking in the Spirit.

E. Points on the Mosaic Law

1. The law is not an instrument of justification (Galatians 2:16, Romans 3:20,28)

2. The law is an instrument of conviction (Romans 3:20, 1Timothy 1:9,10, Galatians 3:21-28).

3. The purpose of the law is to curse mankind (Galatians 3:10,13).

4. The law produces a righteousness but it has no credit with God. It is a fleshly and moral righteousness (Philippians 3:9).

5. The Jews of the Old Testament failed because they tried to use the law as a means of salvation. They used the righteousness from the law as a substitute for the righteousness of God (Romans 9:30-33).

6. The law cannot produce justification (Acts13:39).

III. Righteousness Is by Faith (21–31)

A. Old Testament Salvation

3:21 ¶ But now the righteousness of God apart from the law is revealed, being witnessed by the Law and the Prophets,

But now (contrast) the righteousness of God without (apart from) the law is manifested (revealed clearly), being witnessed (constantly witnessed) by the law and the prophets;

He has always been and will always be the means of salvation for all mankind. This was told through the writings of the Old Testament, the Law (first five books) and the Prophets (major and minor).
Let's look a little more closely at salvation in the Old Testament.

1. There never was nor will be a time, until after the Great White Throne Judgment, when God is not saving mankind. (Romans 10:13, 2 Peter 3:9).

2. The gospel was clearly declared in the Old Testament (Acts 3:18, Romans 1;1-4, 1 Corinthians 15:3,4, Hebrews 4:2).

3. Regardless of the age or dispensation, man has always been saved in the same manner, through faith in the Lord Jesus (Psalm 24:5, Isaiah 9:6, 55:6, 61:10, Acts 4:12).

4. The law was never a means of salvation, even during the Old Testament and the dispensation of the law.

   a) Abraham was saved before the law, by faith in Jesus Christ (Jehovah) (Genesis 15:6, Romans 4:1-4, Galatians 3:6-9).

   b) David was saved during the law, by faith in Jesus Christ (Romans 4:6-8).

   c) We are saved today after the law, by faith in Jesus Christ (John 3:16, Acts 16:31, Romans 10:9,10, Ephesians 2:8,9).

5. The production of faith has always been the means of spirituality regardless of the age or dispensation (Hebrews 11:1,2).

6. Although the object of faith for salvation is the Lord Jesus Christ, His revelation varies with different dispensations (Hebrews 1:1,2).

   a) During innocence, Jesus Christ personally came and taught Adam and Eve.

   b) During Conscience, Human Government and Promise, Jesus Christ spoke in dreams, visions, audible voice and personal appearances.

   c) During the law, Jesus Christ was primarily revealed through shadows: tabernacle, furniture, feast days, fasts, sanitary laws, sacrifices and the operation of the priesthood (Hebrews 10:1).

   d) During the Church Age, the primary means of revelation is the presentation of the word of God (Romans 10:13-17).

7. Many Gentiles were saved in the Old Testament by faith in the Lord Jesus (Exodus 9:20, 12:38, Jonah 3:5, Romans 9:24,25,30-33)

B. Salvation Apart from the Law Is Faith in Jesus Christ

3:22 even the righteousness of God, through faith in Jesus Christ, to all and on all who believe. For there is no difference;

This is the righteousness taught in the Old Testament, faith in Jesus Christ for eternal life and a relationship with God. Jesus is the only means of redemption from sin and for forgiveness of sins. Righteousness is first, to all. Righteousness is something we become. Secondly, righteousness is upon all. It is something we learn to walk in. This verse shows both positional and temporal righteousness. Righteousness is for all who believe. This shows the way man receives God's righteousness. It is by faith.

C. Points on Faith

1. Faith is the only means of human perception which is non meritorious.

2. Faith is described in the word (Hebrews 11:1, 2 Corinthians 4:18).

3. Faith in verb form is transitive, having both a subject and an object. Merit is in the object. Subject (whosoever), object (Christ) believes (action of faith).

4. Faith has a two-fold object:

   a) In salvation the object is Jesus Christ (John 3:16, Acts 16:31).

   b) In Christian growth, discipleship, the object is the word of God (John 8:31-32, 17:17, 2 Corinthians 5:7, Hebrews 11:6).

5. In describing faith, one small amount secures eternal life.

6. Development of faith should be the main goal of every believer (Romans 10:17, Galatians 5:22, Hebrews 4:1-3, 12:2, 1 Peter 1:7).

D. Why Faith Is Needed for Righteousness

3:23 for all have sinned and fall short of the glory of God,

For all (Jew, Gentile, religious, unreligious) have sinned (aorist tense: in Adam) and fall short (present tense) of the glory of God (His righteousness)

3:24 being justified freely by His grace through the redemption that is in Christ Jesus,

Being justified (present tense: vindicated, declared righteous) freely by His grace through the redemption (the cross) that is in Christ Jesus:

3:25 whom God set forth *as* a propitiation by His blood, through faith, to demonstrate His righteousness, because in His forbearance God had passed over the sins that were previously committed,

Whom God set forth (publicly displayed) to be a propitiation (Greek word for the Mercy Seat where the blood of sacrifices was sprinkled) through faith in His blood,

Propitiation also means "satisfaction." God was satisfied with the blood, the work of Jesus on the cross. In animal sacrifices, God had no pleasure or satisfaction. Temporarily, God was appeased as the blood of animals

reminded Him of the eternal blood and redemption which would one day be shed for all mankind. to declare His righteousness for the remission of sins that are past (through faith, to demonstrate His righteousness),
This statement shows that salvation does not come through any part of Jesus' life. You cannot be saved by "following in Jesus' footsteps," "picking up His cross or yours," etc. Salvation comes through the recognition of the death, burial, and resurrection of Jesus Christ.

through the forbearance of God;(because in His forbearance God had passed over the sins that were previously committed),

In the Old Testament, God passed over, but did not ignore the sins of the people. He looked at the animal sacrifices of Israel and anticipated the death of His Son. The people of the Old Testament could be saved, even healed, by looking forward, as God did, to the finished work of Jesus, the eternal sacrifice offered, so no other sacrifice would have to be made. This eternal sacrifice would eternally forgive and remove their sins.

3:26 to demonstrate at the present time His righteousness, that He might be just and the justifier of the one who has faith in Jesus.

To declare (publicly demonstrate) at this present time His righteousness, that He might be (keep on being) just, and the justifier of him who has faith in Jesus. This is the work of the humanity of our Lord Jesus.

3:27 ⁋ Where *is* boasting then? It is excluded. By what law? Of works? No, but by the law of faith.

Where is boasting (pride in self) then? It is excluded. By what law? of works? No: but by the law of faith.

Only the law of faith excludes human boasting. The law of works promotes and encourages boasting.

3:28 Therefore we conclude that a man is justified by faith apart from the deeds of the law.

Therefore we conclude (based on all of Romans to this point) that a man is justified by faith apart from the deeds of the law.

Not only the Ten Commandments, but any system of works of man or religion. Romans 3:23 says there is no difference in the sin nature for all have sinned in Adam, the representative for all mankind. His transgression passed on to all men. The problem is on all and the remedy is for all.

3:29 Or *is He* the God of the Jews only? *Is He* not also the God of the Gentiles? Yes, of the Gentiles also,

Paul is building up to a point. If God is over all races and always has been, then salvation must be the same to all and has always been for all.

3:30 since *there is* one God who will justify the circumcised by faith and the uncircumcised through faith.

Seeing it is one God who shall justify the circumcision (Jew) by faith, and the uncircumcision (Gentile) through faith.

3:31 Do we then make void the law through faith? Certainly not! On the contrary, we establish the law.

Do we then make void (nullify) the law through faith? God forbid (certainly not! On the contrary): yes, we establish (confirm) the law.

Faith fulfills the law. When we accept Jesus Christ by faith, we have done what the law was given for. It was to point to Jesus Christ as the only means of salvation (see Galatians 3:24, 25)

4:1–25 OT Salvation and Spirituality

I. Salvation and Spirituality of Abraham (1–5)

Abraham's spirituality and salvation took place before the law was even taught.

4:1 ¶ What then shall we say that Abraham our father has found according to the flesh?

What shall we say then (I am going to ask an obvious question, don't answer it!) that Abraham our father has found according to the flesh?

Abraham was the physical father of the Jewish nation. Paul is asking a question about the physical Jew, not the spiritual born again believer.

4:2 For if Abraham was justified by works, he has *something* to boast about, but not before God.

Works only allows you to boast before men, not God. God is only moved by our faith as far as salvation.

4:3 For what does the Scripture say? "Abraham believed God, and it was accounted to him for righteousness."

For what does the Scripture say? (Genesis 15:6) Abraham believed God, and it was counted (credited) to him for righteousness.

Abraham is the first of two mentioned, demonstrating salvation and spirituality by faith. Abraham was saved by grace through faith before the law was given. The next, David, will demonstrate God's plan of salvation by grace through faith during the law. The law never could save or produce spirituality. Genesis 15:6 says that Abraham had already believed (Genesis 12 in Ur of the Chaldees) in Jehovah (Jesus Christ). God is revealed through the second member of the Godhead, known as Jehovah in the Old Testament and Jesus in the New (see John 1:18, 6:46, 1 Timothy 6:16, 1 John 4:2).

4:4 Now to him who works, the wages are not counted as grace but as debt.

Now to him who works (legalist), is the reward, not reckoned (counted) as grace but as debt.

The harder you work for salvation, the deeper the rut you dig. The more you borrow, the deeper in debt you go. Also the works will produce a reward, but not a grace reward, not salvation or spirituality.

4:5 ¶ But to him who does not work but believes on Him who justifies the ungodly, his faith is accounted for righteousness,

Salvation is the same for us today as it was for Abraham in his day. Our faith is counted for righteousness before God.

II. Salvation and Spirituality of David (6-8)

David's salvation and spirituality took place while the law was taught.

4:6 just as David also describes the blessedness of the man to whom God imputes righteousness apart from works:

David celebrates the same truth and he lived during the law. Abraham was saved by faith before the law as a Gentile. David was saved by faith during the law as a Jew.

4:7 "Blessed *are those* whose lawless deeds are forgiven, And whose sins are covered;

Saying, Blessed are those whose iniquities (lawless deeds) are forgiven, And whose sins are covered (Psalm 32:1, 2).

In the Old Testament under the law, sins were not removed, but covered. Sins were not removed until the work of Jesus on the cross. All sins before the cross were rolled forward and Jesus took them past, present and future.

4:8 Blessed *is the* man to whom the LORD shall not impute sin."

"Will not impute" is in the subjunctive mood, it is potential. God responds to the individual's faith. This is all from our free will.

III. Abraham's Justification Before Circumcision (9–12)

4:9 ¶ Does this blessedness then *come* upon the circumcised

only, **or upon the uncircumcised also? For we say that faith was accounted to Abraham for righteousness.**

Does this blessedness (salvation by faith) then come on the circumcised (Jew) only, or upon the uncircumcised (Gentile) also? For we say that faith was accounted to Abraham for righteousness.

If Abraham was saved by faith as a Jew, what do the Gentiles do? Does God have another plan of salvation for them? The argument of Paul begins by not calling them Jew or Gentile but circumcised and uncircumcised.

4:10 How then was it accounted? While he was circumcised, or uncircumcised? Not while circumcised, but while uncircumcised.

How (when) was it then reckoned (accounted)? When he was circumcised, or uncircumcised? Not while circumcised, but while uncircumcised.

Paul is asking the question, was Abraham saved when he was circumcised or uncircumcised? It may not seem like a very big question, but it means everything. If Abraham was circumcised, he could be considered a Jew, since the Jewish teaching in Paul's day was this act sealed you as a Jew. If Abraham was uncircumcised he would be a Gentile when saved and circumcised later as a sign of faith. This would all be true since he was called by God from Ur of the Chaldees, making him truly a Gentile. Circumcision would then be a sign and not the means of salvation. Faith saved, not ritual.

4:11 And he received the sign of circumcision, a seal of the righteousness of the faith which *he had while still* **uncircumcised, that he might be the father of all those who believe, though they are uncircumcised, that righteousness might be imputed to them also,**

And he received the sign of circumcision, a seal of the righteousness of the faith which he had while still uncircumcised,

A sign of salvation (which was already reckoned). The parents had the child circumcised (much like child dedication today) as a memorial that they would instruct the child in the ways of the Lord, and it was a sign of faith the child would accept the Lord as savior.

that (in order that) he might be the father (pattern) of all those who be-lieve, though they are uncircumcised, that righteousness might be imput-ed to them also,

Abraham was circumcised as a sign and seal of righteousness which he had already received as uncircumcised. Since righteousness was accounted to Abraham as a Gentile, it is assured that all races can receive Jesus by faith, be saved without works.

4:12 and the father of circumcision to those who not only are of the circumcision, but who also walk in the steps of the faith which our father Abraham *had while still* uncircumcised.

Abraham is not only the example of salvation by faith but also of spiritual-ity by faith. Circumcision did not save Abraham, also it did not make him spiritual. Faith was responsible for both.

IV. Faith and Abraham's Seed (13–25)

A. Not All of Israel Is Israel
Verse 13 Amplified in Romans 9:6-13, telling us not all Israel is Israel.

4:13 ¶ For the promise that he would be the heir of the world *was* not to Abraham or to his seed through the law, but through the righteousness of faith.

For the promise that he would be the heir of the world was not to Abraham or to his seed (Jews) through the law (given only to Jews), but through the righteousness of (produced by) faith.

Paul now begins to tell of the true purpose of the law. If it was not for salvation, and it was given only to one nation, what good is the law then or now?

4:14 For if those who are of the law *are* heirs, faith is made void and the promise made of no effect,

If the Jews were made righteous by keeping the law, what does that do to the rest of the Bible and the rest of humanity? Does it not void the word and cut off Gentiles?

4:15 because the law brings about wrath; for where there is no

law *there is* no transgression.

Paul is using a debaters technique. There can only be transgression of the law where the law exists. If there is no law, no one could transgress. So, the Gentiles should be automatically saved because they never had the law and thus could never transgress what they did not know.

4:16 ¶ Therefore *it is* of faith that *it might* be according to grace, so that the promise might be sure to all the seed, not only to those who are of the law, but also to those who are of the faith of Abraham, who is the father of us all

Therefore (conclusion) it is of faith that it might be according to grace, so that the promise might be sure (secure) to all the seed, not only to those who are of the law (Jews), but also to those who are of the faith of Abraham, who is the father of us all (spiritual father of the Jews and Gentile who exercise faith in Christ).

B. The Seed of Abraham in Scripture

1. Seed: Christ (Galatians 3:16, Hebrews 11:18)

2. Physical Seed: Racial Jews (2 Corinthians 11:22)

3. Spiritual Seed: All born again ones, Jews or Gentiles.

C. Spiritual Life of Abraham

4:17 (as it is written, "I have made you a father of many nations") in the presence of Him whom he believed—God, who gives life to the dead and calls those things which do not exist as though they did;

(As it is written, [Genesis 17:4,5] I have made you a father of many nations) before (in the presence) of Him whom he believed, even God, who quickens (gives life - rebirth of sexual life to Abraham) the dead and calls those things which be not (do not exist) as though they were.

Until now, only the spiritual life of Abraham has been addressed as a result of faith. Now, Abraham and Sarah also receive the ability to have children in their old age. They can now look forward to a spiritual and physical race which will come from them.

4:18 who, contrary to hope, in hope believed, so that he became the father of many nations, according to what was spoken, "So shall your descendants be."

Who against (contrary to) hope believed in hope, that he might become the father of many nations; according to what was spoken, So shall your seed (descendants) be (see Genesis 15:5).

Beyond a natural hope (no ability to have children) Abraham found supernatural hope through the promises of God. God's word not only produces faith in us, but a hope for the future.

4:19 And not being weak in faith, he did not consider his own body, already dead (since he was about a hundred years old), and the deadness of Sarah's womb.

And not being weak in faith, he considered not (did not reflect on) his own body, already dead when he was about a hundred years old (99), neither the deadness of Sarah's womb.

This verse says that Abraham did not consider his own body and the deadness of Sarah's womb and did not waver at the promise of God.
However, this does not mean Abraham and Sarah did not look at the natural dilemma they were in. They did and even laughed at the promise of God when it was first given. They put God's promise above the sight of their eyes and natural thoughts of doubt.

4:20 He did not waver at the promise of God through unbelief, but was strengthened in faith, giving glory to God,

Not only did Abraham not stagger in faith, he increased in faith. This means he had to meditate on the promise of God in the meantime because faith comes by hearing. When we rest on God's promises and do not stagger in unbelief, we always give God glory.

4:21 and being fully convinced that what He had promised He was also able to perform.

And being fully persuaded (convinced) that what He (God) had (aorist: once and for all) promised He was also able to perform (make good).

When God first spoke to Abraham, he took a step of faith to trust in God. By meditating on the word, Abraham became fully convinced of God's promise to him despite the doubts of his own mind and opinions of men.

4:22 And therefore "it was accounted to him for righteousness."

And therefore it (faith) was imputed (accounted) to him for righteousness.

Abraham's faith began at salvation and increased to see a child and a nation formed. Faith brought him spiritual righteousness at salvation and temporal righteousness for daily life afterward.

D. Final Conclusion
Verses 23 through 25 are the end of the parenthesis begun in verse 17.

4:23-24 ¶ Now it was not written for his sake alone that it was imputed to him, 24 but also for us. It shall be imputed to us who believe in Him who raised up Jesus our Lord from the dead,

This is believing in the work of the Father, even though we believe in Jesus Christ. Part of our faith is to believe in the Father who raised Jesus from the dead (John 5:24, Romans 10:9-10).

4:25 who was delivered up because of our offenses, and was raised because of our justification.

Who (Jesus) was delivered up for (because of) our offenses, and was raised for (because of) our justification.

Our sins sent Jesus to the cross and our justification caused Him to be resurrected. He was not raised to justify us, but because we were already justified. Having obtained our righteousness caused Jesus to be raised from the dead.

5:1–21 Much More Grace

After salvation, grace continues as the means of spirituality.

I. Four Results of Justification (1-5)

A. Peace

> **5:1 ¶ Therefore, having been justified by faith, we have peace with God through our Lord Jesus Christ,**

Therefore (summary of justification from Romans 4:25) being justified by faith, we have peace (reconciliation) with God through our Lord Jesus Christ:

Peace can only come through faith in Jesus Christ. Peace is supernatural and is found in no other place than in Christ at salvation and in His word afterwards.
Peace is also reconciliation. Let's look a little more closely at reconciliation.

1. Reconciliation is peace with God because of the removal of the barrier between God and man.

2. Peace is the result of man's response by faith to the grace of God (Romans 5:1).

3. Therefore, peace is a synonym for reconciliation.

4. On the cross, Jesus became sin for us and removed it as the barrier between God and man.

5. Since Jesus became sin, He is the only barrier to reconciliation today. Peace between us and God comes through our acceptance or rejection of Him (Romans 5:10).

6. The means of reconciliation is given in Ephesians 2:14-18.

7. The cross is the point of reconciliation for God (Colossians 1:20).

8. The results of reconciliation are given in Colossians 1:21,22.

9. Once a person is reconciled, he becomes a minister of reconciliation
(2 Corinthians 5:18,19).

10. Reconciliation, the gospel of peace, is the believer's primary message (Isaiah 52:7, Romans 10:15, Ephesians 6:15).

B. Eternal Security

5:2 through whom also we have access by faith into this grace in which we stand, and rejoice in hope of the glory of God.

By (through) whom (Christ) we also have access by faith into this grace wherein we stand, and rejoice in hope of the glory of God.

Grace never stops from the moment of salvation but becomes the access, the path into the presence of God (Hebrews 4:16) and the "more grace" prepared for us (James 4:6).

C. Blessing in Pressure

5:3 And not only that, but we also glory in tribulations, knowing that tribulation produces perseverance;

And not only that, but we also glory in tribulations, knowing that tribulation works out (produces) patience (perseverance);

Knowledge is a major key in the Christian life to handling the problems and trials we all face after salvation. Only by understanding scripture can we offer glory and praise to God in the middle of a battle, knowing God will bring us through and strengthen us in the meantime. Coming through problems produces and increases patience in our life. Tribulation "works out" patience (*katergozomai*). Patience is already in us as a fruit of the Holy Spirit and is brought to the surface for us and others to see as we come through troubles of life. Problems do not produce maturity. If this was true, all believers would be mature. Maturity is produced as we use the word of God in the problems of life.

5:4 and perseverance, character; and character, hope.

And patience (perseverance), experience (character); and experience (character), hope.

Patience is alive. It continues to produce character in our life which cannot be shaken and a new hope for the future. For example, what God did for us this time, bringing us through a major problem, will happen again.

D. Love from the Holy Spirit

5:5 Now hope does not disappoint, because the love of God has been poured out in our hearts by the Holy Spirit who was

given to us.

And hope makes us not ashamed (does not disappoint); because the love of God is shed abroad (has been poured out or liberally and distributed) in our hearts by the Holy Spirit which was given to us.

Our walk of faith builds up a testimony in us and gives us a confidence before the world that cannot be shaken. We also give out God's love through the Holy Spirit who lives in us.

II. Christ and Our Condition (6–8)

A. Our Condition

1. Unrighteous
2. Sinners
3. Enemies of God

5:6 ¶ For when we were still without strength, in due time Christ died for the ungodly.

For when we were still without strength (*dunamis:* power to save ourselves), in due (proper) time Christ died for the ungodly.

Jesus picked a time to die for us when we had nothing to offer Him: racial correctness, personal righteousness or strength to save ourselves. All glory, for everything, goes to God and His plan.

B. Christ's Motivation
Verse 7 is an analogy of love.

5:7 For scarcely for a righteous man will one die; yet perhaps for a good man someone would even dare to die.

For scarcely (with difficulty) for a righteous (moral) man will one die; yet peradventure (perhaps) for a good (moral, generous) man some would even dare to die.

This is a display of human love and its qualifications. We might offer ourselves in the place of someone who is moral or benevolent and has been wrongly accused. But would we offer ourselves in exchange for a criminal or morally bankrupt person who robs, contributes little, or gives nothing to society.

5:8 But God demonstrates His own love toward us, in that while we were still sinners, Christ died for us.

But (contrast) God commends (demonstrates or offers) His love toward us, in that while we were yet sinners, Christ died for us.

This is the contrast of divine love and human love. Our love, human love, is selective in the extent to which we would offer ourselves. Only God's love, divine love, would offer His own spotless, sinless Son in exchange for a lost and sinful population which had done no good in God's sight, nor ever could. Jesus died for those who hated Him.

III. Justification and Reconciliation (9–11)

A. Deliverance by Justification
Verse 9 is the first of three places the phrase "much more" is used to contrast our past, sinful state with our present, redeemed one. The first "much more" is Deliverance by Justification.

5:9 Much more then, having now been justified by His blood, we shall be saved from wrath through Him.

Much more then, having now been justified (vindicated) by His blood, we shall be saved (future deliverance) from wrath (Romans 8:1, no condemnation) through Him.

This includes the wrath of the Tribulation as well as hell and the lake of fire.

B. Result of Reconciliation
Verse 10 is the second "much more": the result of reconciliation. Verses 10 and 11 both teach that reconciliation is the removal of the barrier between God and man.

5:10 For if when we were enemies we were reconciled to God through the death of His Son, much more, having been reconciled, we shall be saved by His life.

For if when we were enemies we were reconciled (aorist, passive: once and for all we received reconciliation) to God through the death of His Son, much more, having been reconciled, we shall be saved (ultimately) by His life.

C. Points on Reconciliation

1. Jesus Christ is the agent of reconciliation (Romans 5:10).

2. The believer is the minister of reconciliation (2 Corinthians 5:18,19).

3. Mechanics of removing the barrier (Ephesians 2:16).

4. The cross is the point of reconciliation (Colossians 1:20).

5. Ultimate sanctification is the result of reconciliation (Colossians 1:21, 22).

5:11 And not only *that*, but we also rejoice in God through our Lord Jesus Christ, through whom we have now received the reconciliation.

And not only that (future) but we also (now) rejoice in God through our Lord Jesus Christ, through whom we have now received the atonement (reconciliation).

Reconciliation, once understood, not only brings great hope and relief for the future but also joy for the present.

IV. The First and Last (12–21)

A. The First Adam

5:12 ¶ Therefore, just as through one man sin entered the world, and death through sin, and thus death spread to all men, because all sinned—

Therefore, just as by one man (Adam) sin (nature of the flesh) entered the world, SIN (singular) refers to the nature of the flesh. SINS (plural) refer to personal sins or acts which come from the nature of the flesh, sin. And thus death (spiritual) spread to all men, because all sinned.

Adam is the head, the representative, of all mankind. What happened in him, happened in us. When he fell, we all fell. Adam became a sinner because he sinned. We sin because we are a sinner. His act produced the sin nature. Our sin nature produces the acts. We do not become a sinner because we sin. We are born into sin because of Adam's sin. His act and curse spread to all men. The first thing which entered into Adam was the nature of the flesh, sin. Through the nature of the flesh, spiritual death entered. We are born into this world with the nature of the flesh and spiritual death. Adam died from the outside in. Jesus, the last Adam, came to redeem us. He changes what Adam did to us, from the inside out. We are presently made spiritually alive, but left with the nature of the flesh. This will be removed at physical death or the Rapture of the Church when we have a resurrection body, free from the flesh nature. (Victory over the flesh in this life will be the theme of chapter 8.)

Let's look a little more closely at the sin nature.

1. The sin nature is that tendency dictating toward the soul to act independently of God (Romans 7:23).

2. The first ones to receive a sin nature were Adam and Eve. By acting independently of God's will they received the sin nature (sin-singular). They in turn passed in on through physical birth to their children, so that today ALL members of the human race are born with this nature (Psalm 51:5, Romans 5:12).

3. All personal sins come from the sin nature whether the person is a believer or unbeliever.

4. All good deeds of the unbeliever (Isaiah 64:6, Titus 3:5), or the carnal believer (Romans 8:8), come from the sin nature and do not please God. These deeds are human good.

5. The believer continues to possess a sin nature after the new birth, but is no longer under its domination (Romans 6).

6. If the believer walks according to the new nature, the inward man, the recreated human spirit, he is controlled by the Holy Spirit and not the sin nature (Romans 6:12-14, 8:4,5, Galatians 5:16).

7. The location of the sin nature is the body, the only part of the believer still under the curse and yet to be redeemed (Romans 6:6,12,13, 7:5,23,24).

8. Terms used in scripture to describe the sin nature:

   a) Sin (singular in contrast to sins which come from sin) (Psalm 51:5, Romans 5:12, Romans 7:14, 1 John 1:8, Romans 6:1)

   b) Flesh (emphasis on its location, the body) (Romans 7:18, Romans 8:8, Romans 13:14, Galatians 5:16-21, Ephesians 2:3)

   c) Old Man (it arrived with natural birth from Adam) (Romans 6:6, Ephesians 4:22, Colossians 3:5-9)

   d) Spirit (James 4:5)

5:13 (For until the law sin was in the world, but sin is not imputed when there is no law.

(For until the law sin [the flesh] was in the world, but sin is not imputed [held against us] when there is no law.

Until the Mosaic Law came, people sinned but had no revelation of why they sinned. The culprit had to be revealed before the answer could be shown. The Law of Moses would do both. Only a few things were held against man before the law. The law revealed the problem with man (sin nature of the flesh) and the answer which is atonement through Jesus' blood.

5:14 Nevertheless death reigned from Adam to Moses, even over those who had not sinned according to the likeness of the transgression of Adam, who is a type of Him who was to come.

Nevertheless death [spiritual] reigned from Adam to Moses, even over those who had not sinned according to the likeness of the transgression of Adam, who is a type of Him who was to come.

Even though the flesh was not understood, spiritual death in man reigned over him, even though we had not sinned in the same manner as Adam. Adam sinned and became spiritually dead. We are spiritually dead and so we sin. Adam is a type of Jesus, the One who was to come. Adam was perfect, spiritually alive, was tempted, fell for it, and transgressed, throwing us into spiritual death and sins. Jesus came, like Adam, spiritually alive, was tempted, yet did not yield to the temptation. He died in our place, without any personal sin for those who were born into spiritual death and sins. Jesus was able to undo what Adam had done. The world had no choice to be born into sin, but has a choice to get out of it. Faith in Jesus Christ reconciles us back to God and reinstates us into right standing with God even though we still possess the nature of the flesh.

B. The Last Adam: Jesus
In verse 14, Adam and Jesus are compared. In verse 15, they are contrasted. Verse 15 is the third "much more": the grace of salvation.

5:15 But the free gift *is* not like the offense. For if by the one man's offense many died, much more the grace of God and the gift by the grace of the one Man, Jesus Christ, abounded

to many.

God's free gift of salvation is not at all to be compared to the trespass. The trespass of Adam killed all men. The grace of God through Jesus Christ resurrects all men who believe. Also the death of Adam was passed to all men without our choice. We have been given a choice in gaining eternal life, "whosoever will may come." "In Adam all die, so in Christ shall all be made alive."

5:16 And the gift *is* not like *that which came* through the one who sinned. For the judgment *which came* from one offense resulted in condemnation, but the free gift *which came* from many offenses *resulted* in justification.

Adam passed on spiritual death to all after he committed one transgression. We receive reconciliation freely even after committing many transgressions.

5:17 For if by the one man's offense death reigned through the one, much more those who receive abundance of grace and of the gift of righteousness will reign in life through the One, Jesus Christ.)

For if by one man's offense death reigned [as king] by one [Adam], much more they who receive [the act of faith] abundance of grace and of the gift of righteousness will reign in life through the One, Jesus Christ.)

Grace and faith go hand in hand (Ephesians 2:8). Whatever God offers in grace, we must receive by faith.
Verse 17 mentions two "much mores": the abundance of grace and the gift of righteousness.

C. The Two Acts of Adam and Jesus
Verse 18 continues the sentence begun in verse 12.

5:18 ¶ Therefore, as through one man's offense *judgment came* to all men, resulting in condemnation, even so through one Man's righteous act *the free gift came* to all men, resulting in justification of life.

Therefore, as by to offence of one (Adam) judgment came upon all men to (resulting in) condemnation, even so by the righteousness of One (Jesus

Christ) the free gift came to all men, unto (resulting in) justification of life.

D. The Wills of Adam and Jesus

5:19 For as by one man's disobedience many were made sinners, so also by one Man's obedience many will be made righteous.

For as by one man's disobedience many were made (appointed) sinners, so also by one Man's obedience many will be made righteous.

Adam willfully chose to disobey God. Jesus willfully chose to obey God. The results from both have affected multitudes.

5:20 ¶ Moreover the law entered that the offense might abound. But where sin abounded, grace abounded much more,

"Entered" is a theatrical term for a minor actor who entered the stage only until the major actor arrived. Then the minor actor exited. The law came in to play a minor part to expose the offense, the problem, sin. Once sin, the villain, was exposed, grace, the hero, much more abounded.

E. The Problem and the Solution

The dual purpose of the law was to expose the problem, the flesh, and reveal the answer, Jesus Christ.

5:21 so that as sin reigned in death, even so grace might reign through righteousness to eternal life through Jesus Christ our Lord.

That as sin reigned (resulting) unto death, even so might grace reign through righteousness unto eternal life through Jesus Christ our Lord.

The nature of the flesh has full reign in a person who is spiritually dead. But righteousness can have full reign in a person who is spiritually alive, born again and walking in the power of the Holy Spirit.

6:1–23 Temporal Truth or Experiential Sanctification

Chapter 6 of Romans the application of positional truth to the experiences of life, the daily development of sanctification and the walk of faith. It is called "walking in newness of life" (v. 4). It is a culmination of five chapters and asks a question in view of all we have learned to this point. What about the sin nature after we are born again? Do we still have it? Does it maintain in control of our life if we do have it? Chapter 6 gives the doctrine of victory over the flesh.

I. The Question of Continuing Sin (1)

6:1 ¶ What shall we say then? Shall we continue in sin that grace may abound?

What shall we say then? Shall we continue in sin (under its domination) that grace may abound?

Now that we are born again, shall we continually live by the dictates of the flesh because we are under grace?

II. The Answer to Continuing Sin (2-14)

A. Abounding Grace

The first verse of chapter 6 amplifies Romans 5:20. Where sin abounded, grace did *much more abound.*

6:2 Certainly not! How shall we who died to sin live any longer in it?

God forbid (Certainly not!) How shall we who are dead to sin (sin nature) live any longer in it?

This is bringing up verse 7 where the sin nature died and we are free to marry another. This is positional and eternal sanctification received at salvation. We died to sin, our former husband, at the new birth, but he did not die to us.

B. Baptism

6:3 Or do you not know that as many of us as were baptized into Christ Jesus were baptized into His death?

Paul reminds believers that they know (or should know) certain truths three times in this chapter (vv. 3,6,9).

6:4 Therefore we were buried with Him through baptism into death, that just as Christ was raised from the dead by the glory of the Father, even so we also should walk in newness of life.

Therefore (conclusion) we were buried with Him by baptism into death: that just as Christ was raised from the dead by the glory of the Father, even so we also should walk in newness of life.

Let's take an in-depth look at the word "baptism."

1. From the Greek word *baptizo* meaning:

    a) To dip (Luke 16:24, John 13:26, Revelation 19:13)

    b) To wash (Mark 7:4)

2. Baptism always typifies the passing of something old and entering into the new.

3. Baptism always denotes identification which is positional truth.

4. There are seven types of baptism found in the Bible.

    a) Baptism of followers of John the Baptist into water (Matthew 3:11, Mark 1:8, Luke 3:3, 7:29,30, John 1:31).

    1) This was a symbol of following the will of God for the coming of Jesus' ministry.

    2) The water represented the passing of one time period (Israel) and the beginning of a new (Church).

    b) Baptism of Jesus into water (John 3:22, 4:1,2)

    1) This was an outward sign of the consecration of Jesus to do the will of the Father, go to the cross and die for the sins of the world.

    2) The water represented the end of finding the will of God and the beginning of doing it.

    c) Christian baptism into water (Matthew 28:19, Mark 16:16, Acts 2:38-41, 1 Corinthians 1:13,14).

1) This is an outward display of our acceptance of Jesus Christ as Savior.

2) The water represents death to the old life and resurrection to the new.

d) Jesus' baptism of the cup (suffering) (Matthew 20:22, Luke 12:50)

1) This was the acceptance of Jesus to bear the sins of the world.

2) The earthly ministry of Jesus had come to an end and now was the time to accomplish the plan of redemption.

e) Baptism of Moses (1 Corinthians 10:1,2)

1) This was the passage through the Red Sea.

2) This represented the putting off of the yoke of Egypt and crossing over into the plan of God.

f) Baptism into Christ and His body (Romans 6:3-7, 1 Corinthians 12:13, Galatians 3:27, Ephesians 4:5, Colossians 2:12).

1) This is accomplished by the Holy Spirit at the new birth (1 Corinthians 12:13).

2) This is the true death of the old life and coming of the new.

g) Baptism or infilling of the Holy Spirit (Matthew 3:11, Acts 1:5,8).

1) This baptism brings power for Christian service.

2) This is a symbol of death to the energy of the flesh and entrance into the life of the supernatural power of the Holy Spirit.

5. The baptism of Romans 6:3 is baptism into Christ, the new birth.

a) This baptism was not found in the Old Testament.

b) Jesus prophesied of it. "At that day you shall know that I am in the Father, and you in me, and I in you" (John 14:20).

c) It occurred for the first time at Pentecost.

d) Salvation is the entrance into this baptism.

e) This baptism is unseen and unfelt. It is discovered by knowledge.

"we should walk.." It us up to us whether we apply the word or not. We should walk in the new life of the Spirit. This shows there is victory over the flesh so we can walk in the Spirit. Our temporal life (walk) can and should match our position in Christ.

This baptism was not around in the Old Testament. It was first prophesied by Jesus (John 14:20). It occurred for the first time at Pentecost. It occurs in us at salvation and we become one with Christ and each other as believers (1 Corinthians 12:13, Ephesians 4:5). This baptism is the basis for positional truth (Ephesians 1:3-14). It is an event, not an experience or feeling.

> **6:5 ¶ For if we have been united together in the likeness of His death, certainly we also shall be *in the likeness* of *His* resurrection,**

This verse amplifies baptism in verse 3. This is the positional death, burial and resurrection of our salvation.
Verse 6 is the second knowledge phrase (along with vv. 6 and 9).

> **6:6 knowing this, that our old man was crucified with *Him*, that the body of sin might be done away with, that we should no longer be slaves of sin.**

Knowing this, that our old man (flesh, sin nature) was crucified with Him, that the body of sin might be done away with, that we should no longer be slaves of sin.

This verse is an introduction to chapter 7 where the flesh will be taught as the first husband and the old man.

C. Names for the Sin Nature

1. Flesh: John 3:6, Galatians 5:16

2. Old man: Ephesians 4:22, Romans 6:6

3. Heart of man: Jeremiah 17:9

4. Sin (singular): Romans 7:14,17, 1 John 1:8

This is the first of many verses describing the location of the flesh.
The sin nature is part of the body. This is why it is called the "body of sin." It dwells in our "members" (Romans 7:5). We can render the flesh inoperative until the day our body is dead or redeemed at the Rapture of the Church. Just like pulling the coil wire from a distributor of a car, the car is rendered inoperative or powerless, but not destroyed. In this way the flesh is still present, but powerless and we do not serve it.

> **6:7 For he who has died has been freed from sin.**

For he who has died has been freed from sin (flesh).

This is retroactive positional truth. God did not see our flesh as dead when we were born again, but at the cross when Jesus said, "it is finished." Death nullifies all obligations of life. This will be seen for its spiritual truth in the verses to come.

6:8 Now if we died with Christ, we believe that we shall also live with Him,

Now if we died with Christ (and we did), we believe that we shall also live with Him.

This verse is our present and future positional truth, all based on Jesus' death. We live now with Him and in the future we will be with Him in heaven.
Verse 9 is the third knowledge phrase (along with vv. 3 and 6).

6:9 knowing that Christ, having been raised from the dead, dies no more. Death no longer has dominion over Him.

Knowing that Christ, having been raised from the dead, dies no more; death no longer has dominion (rulership) over Him.

Jesus solved not only personal sins, but also every aspect of the flesh nature's control over our lives.

6:10 For *the death* that He died, He died to sin once for all; but *the life* that He lives, He lives to God.

Jesus died, not only to save us from hell, but also to save us daily from the power of the flesh. Jesus died to sin, without possessing the sin nature or ever being under its control. He did it for us. He now lives to God in a place where there is no sin nature or personal sins. He did this for us so we too can be free from the flesh and live in a place in this life, free from the control of sin and personal sins.

6:11 Likewise you also, reckon yourselves to be dead indeed to sin, but alive to God in Christ Jesus our Lord.

Likewise reckon (calculate, count as done) you also, yourselves to be dead indeed to sin, but alive to God through Christ Jesus our Lord.

Jesus is our example and power for life. He did not die for Himself, but for us. We can use the power of the Holy Spirit to walk free from the power of the flesh and walk in newness of life toward God. From death, we now live in resurrection.

6:12 ¶ Therefore do not let sin reign in your mortal body, that you should obey it in its lusts.

Again, the sin nature is in our mortal body. If the sin nature reigns, we live in obedience to it. To reign is to be a king and someone must bow.
The lusts of the sin nature are good and evil, not just sins, but good deeds also. These good deeds do not have God's approval. The energy of the flesh can produce both. The energy of the Holy Spirit can only produce divine good — good works acceptable to God.

6:13 And do not present your members as instruments of unrighteousness to sin, but present yourselves to God as being alive from the dead, and your members as instruments of righteousness to God.

Our "members" are our body. When we live in the power of the Holy Spirit, our body becomes a servant living for God as His channel of righteousness in this earth.

6:14 For sin shall not have dominion over you, for you are not under law but under grace.

For sin (the flesh) shall not have dominion over you, for you are not under the law but under grace.

God's intention is for us to live free from the power of sin. Now that we have been released from the law at salvation, we should walk free from the flesh each day afterward. The law works through the flesh. Grace works through our recreated spirit. The choice to live under the control of the flesh, the law, or under the control of the Spirit, grace, is up to us.

III. The Question of Occasional Sin (15)

6:15 ¶ What then? Shall we sin because we are not under law but under grace? Certainly not!

Since we are under grace, is grace a license to sin? Or, can we just sin occasionally? The answer to both is, emphatically not.

IV. The Answer for Occasional Sin (16–23)

6:16 Do you not know that to whom you present yourselves slaves to obey, you are that one's slaves whom you obey, whether of sin *leading* to death, or of obedience *leading* to righteousness?

Do you not know that to whom you present yourselves servants to obey, you are that one's slaves whom you obey, whether of sin leading (producing) to death (temporal), or of obedience leading to (producing) righteousness?

This verse, along with others, shows us that only knowledge can keep us from sin and cause us to mature. We are a slave either way in our Christian life, either to our spirit or the flesh. Only the Holy Spirit, working through our human spirit, can make us a slave possessing true freedom. When we are carnal, we are a slave to the flesh. When we are spiritual, we are a slave to our spirit and the Holy Spirit. Carnality produces death doomed results. Spirituality produces eternally living results.

A. Positional Deliverance

6:17 But God be thanked that *though* you were slaves of sin, yet you obeyed from the heart that form of doctrine to which you were delivered.

But God be thanked that though you were servants of sin (the flesh), yet you obeyed from the heart that form (sum or total) of doctrine (teaching) which was delivered to you.

The only way to temporal sanctification is to keep your eyes on positional sanctification. You can become more righteous in your daily life as you keep your eyes on positional righteousness (Colossians 3:1- 3). This type of truth is delivered, which shows the importance of a pastor or teacher.

6:18 And having been set free from sin, you became slaves of righteousness.

And having been (becoming) set free from sin (flesh, sin nature), you became the servants of righteousness.

We have been delivered not only from the bondage of sin, but also the bondage to sin.

B. Being Yielded

6:19 I speak in human *terms* because of the weakness of your flesh. For just as you presented your members as slaves of uncleanness, and of lawlessness *leading* to *more* lawlessness, so now present your members as slaves *of* righteousness for holiness.

I speak after the manner of men (human viewpoint) because of the infirmity (weakness) of your flesh (sin nature). For just as you yielded (presented) your members as servants (slaves) of uncleanness, and of Iniquity (lawlessness) leading to more lawlessness, so now yield (present) your members as servants of righteousness (the new nature) for (resulting in) holiness.

The sin nature, the flesh, is called unclean and iniquity. Since everything produces after its own kind, so the sin nature produces acts of iniquity from the source or nature of iniquity. Spiritual life produces holiness (sanctification in our daily life).

Verse 20 introduces the theme of chapter 7. We have been released from one husband to remarry another, from sin to righteousness.

6:20 ¶ For when you were slaves of sin, you were free in regard to righteousness.

For when you were slaves of sin (a sinner), you were free in regard to righteousness.

When you were a sinner, you could not produce righteousness. It is impossible for an unbeliever to produce divine good. He can only produce human good.

C. Points on Human Good

1. In the unbeliever, all human works are judged at the Great White Throne Judgment (Revelation 20:12,13 - according to their works)

2. For the believer, all human good is judged at the Judgment Seat Of Christ (1 Corinthians 3:12 - wood, hay, stubble...)

6:21 What fruit did you have then in the things of which you are now ashamed? For the end of those things *is* death.

The unbeliever can produce no fruit. He is a fruitless tree. The final result of a sinner's life is spiritual separation from God for eternity.

6:22 But now having been set free from sin, and having become slaves of God, you have your fruit to holiness, and the end, everlasting life.

But now (after salvation) having been set free from sin (sin nature, flesh), and having become servants of God, you have your fruit to (resulting in) holiness, and the end, everlasting life.

6:23 For the wages of sin *is* death, but the gift of God *is* eternal life in Christ Jesus our Lord.

For the wages of sin is death (spiritual death followed by the second death), but the gift of God is eternal life through (in) Jesus Christ our Lord.

A sinner cannot produce fruit. Galatians 5 calls flesh production as works and spiritual production as fruit. Unbelievers cannot produce fruit, but works. Works demand wages.

The sin nature gives a pay check or a recompense for work done. The contrast between the believer and unbeliever is gift versus wages. Wages are worked for, a gift is freely received.

7:1–25 Two Husbands and Two Marriage Counselors

The two marriages and the two husbands are a type of the sin nature or the flesh, and the Lord Jesus Christ. The two counselors are a type of the Mosaic Law and the Holy Spirit. The children of the marriage are the works of the flesh (Galatians 5:19-21) and the fruit of the Spirit (Galatians 5:22,23).

I. First Husband: Sin (1–3)

7:1 ⁋ Or do you not know, brethren (for I speak to those who know the law), that the law has dominion over a man as long as he lives?

The Roman believers know the Mosaic Law but are ignorant of the new law or the life of Christ Jesus. The analogy being drawn from this passage is that once you were a pig married to a pig. Now you are a lamb married to a lamb. But it is embarrassing to be a lamb and produce pig children. The believer out of fellowship, under the control of the flesh, produces pigs. You have been having fellowship with your old husband in the mud puddle. You are dead to the pig and married to the lamb. He is not dead to you he comes courting now and then to woo you. Reckon yourself to be dead to sin (see Romans 6:11).

7:2 For the woman who has a husband is bound by the law to *her* husband as long as he lives. But if the husband dies, she is released from the law of *her* husband.

We are the wife. We always assume the nature and name of the husband. He is the head and we cannot have two heads. We were once bound by law to the previous husband when we were unbelievers.

7:3 So then if, while *her* husband lives, she marries another man, she will be called an adulteress; but if her husband dies, she is free from that law, so that she is no adulteress, though she has married another man.

So then if, while her husband (present husband) lives, she marries another man, she will be called an adulteress; but if her husband dies, she is free from that law, so that she is no adulteress, though she has married another man.

Paul is saying that the believer (married to Jesus) who is carnal is committing adultery (living in domination to the flesh or sin nature). When we were born again, the first husband died to us and we are free from him. We received Jesus as our new husband. This is legal and we are not an adulteress. These verses are just an analogy. The husband dying here is only representative of what happens to us spiritually. In reality, the husband did not die, the wife died, and has come back to life, been resurrected, and is free to remarry. We died to the sin nature and we are to count it as dead to us. This will be brought out in verse 4.

II. Second Husband: Jesus Christ (4–6)

7:4 Therefore, my brethren, you also have become dead to the law through the body of Christ, that you may be married to another—to Him who was raised from the dead, that we should bear fruit to God.

Your old husband is freed from you because you died. Now we can bring forth new children, lambs, instead of pigs. Fruit to God is our children which we produce from our new husband.

7:5 For when we were in the flesh, the sinful passions which were aroused by the law were at work in our members to bear fruit to death.

For when we were in the flesh (married to the first husband), the sinful passions which were aroused by the law were at work in our members to bear fruit to death.

The productions or acts of sins were only supposed to be made when we were sinners, married to the old husband. We produced sinful acts because it was our nature. Again, this nature is found in our bodies, our members.

7:6 But now we have been delivered from the law, having died to what we were held by, so that we should serve in the newness of the Spirit and not *in* the oldness of the letter.

The law is the marriage counselor in verse 5 "...the motions of sins which were by the law." In the new creation, our spirit is made new, not our body. The new life is lived from the inside out or from our spirit.

The old life was from the outside in. But when we live by the flesh as believers, we imitate the unbeliever instead of God (Galatians 5:14-25).

The works of the flesh are the children of the first marriage. The children are adultery, drunkenness, etc. The fruit of the spirit are the children of the second marriage, love, joy, peace, etc. Both sets of children are from Abraham. The children of the law are Ishmael, who came from Hagar, the law, or the flesh. The children of the new covenant are Isaac, who came from Sarah, the new covenant, or the spirit. Ishmael represents the production of the law and Isaac the production of grace.

Assumption is refuted. If the law causes me to sin and always condemns me, then apparently the law must be sin. NO! The law was used to expose my problem. It comes from God so it cannot be sinful. Every good and perfect gift comes from God.

III. The Law (5–25)

A. Uncovers Sin

> 7:7 ¶ What shall we say then? *Is* the law sin? Certainly not! On the contrary, I would not have known sin except through the law. For I would not have known covetousness unless the law had said, "You shall not covet."

In the light of what we have just studied, we were under sin and alive to the law. The law was holy, just and good, but we were not. We were sold under the sin nature. We needed something to expose the problem that kept us in sin and then an answer to take us out of the problem. That was the purpose of the law. I did not know I had covetousness, or lust, until I read the law which told me not to covet (see Exodus 20:17).

B. Five Kinds of Lust

1. Power Lust: Wanting to run the show.

2. Approbation Lust: Wanting to be seen of men and appreciated

3. Ego Lust: Pride, love of self

4. Material Lust: Love of money and the things of life

5. Sexual Lust: Lasciviousness

7:8 But sin, taking opportunity by the commandment, produced in me all *manner of evil* desire. For apart from the law sin *was* dead.

But sin (flesh), taking opportunity by the commandment, wrought (produced) in me all manner of concupiscence (evil desire). For without the law sin was dead (inoperative).

The base of operation of the flesh nature is the law. Until the law was given, this nature was present, but dead, dormant.

7:9 I was alive once without the law, but when the commandment came, sin revived and I died.

I was alive without the law, but when I learned its commandments, the sin nature came to life and I lost the battle. I died to my own control of my life. I found out how helpless I was to save myself when the law came. My enemy, the flesh, was far greater than my natural strength.

7:10 And the commandment, which *was* to *bring* life, I found to *bring* death.

The law was originally designed to give life, but every time it tried to produce life, it aroused the sin nature, the flesh. And what was supposed to give life, brought death.

7:11 For sin, taking occasion by the commandment, deceived me, and by it killed *me*.

The sin nature, seized the commandment, deceived me into thinking I could save myself. Yet, instead of having life, I died.

7:12 Therefore the law *is* holy, and the commandment holy and just and good.

God is holy, just and good. What He gives to us is also holy, just and good. This includes the law. My problem was, I was not holy, just and good. I discovered the law was not my answer. It first revealed my problem, the flesh. Next, it revealed my answer, Jesus Christ. The law is designed for a righteous man, walking in righteousness. Only he can fulfill the righteousness found in the law. When the law meets an unrighteous man or a carnal Christian, under the control of the flesh, it can only magnify his problems.

C. True Ministry of the Law

7:13 ¶ Has then what is good become death to me? Certainly not! But sin, that it might appear sin, was producing death in me through what is good, so that sin through the commandment might become exceedingly sinful.

Did the law kill me? NO! When the law came, and I tried to keep it, it was revealed for what it really is. It is a base of operation for the sin nature. The law energizes the flesh. Spiritual death was already working in me using the law for its strength. We become exceedingly sinful, produce acts and deeds of sin, because of sin resident in our body. We are not sinners because we sin. We sin because we are sinners.

7:14 For we know that the law is spiritual, but I am carnal, sold under sin.

The law is holy, just and good, but It takes something spiritual to operate or fulfill it. I as a human being am powerless to operate the law properly. This is because in myself I am carnal, sold under sin, enslaved under the mastery of the sin nature. I am a slave at any moment to the spirit or flesh (v. 16).

7:15 For what I am doing, I do not understand. For what I will to do, that I do not practice; but what I hate, that I do.

For what I am doing (what is working out of me), I do not understand (approve of). For what I will (desire) to do, that I do not practice; but what I hate, that I do (keep on doing).

What I want to do, I do sometimes, but I cannot keep it up as a way of life. I do not practice my desires. I am powerless in myself to live a righteous life, fulfilling the law.

7:16 If, then, I do what I will not to do, I agree with the law that *it is* good.

If then, I do what I will (desire) not to do, I agree with (endorse) the law that it is good (correct).

Whenever I commit sin, I am proving that the law is correct. It is designed to show that I am carnal, a sinner. When I sin, I am acknowledging that fact whether I want to admit it or not.

7:17 But now, *it is* no longer I who do it, but sin that dwells in me.

But now (when I am carnal), it is no longer I who do it (work it out), but sin that dwells in me.

Once I make a decision to sin, the sin nature arises and dominates me and is not working with me. I am working with it. It has me as a master over a slave.

7:18 For I know that in me (that is, in my flesh) nothing good dwells; for to will is present with me, but *how* to perform what is good I do not find.

Paul now locates the problem area, the body. When Paul says, "sin in me," he is not referring to the inner man, the heart. He is speaking of the outward man, the human body. It still carries the curse from Adam. We brought it over from our old life, before salvation. It will not be removed until physical death or the Rapture. The resurrection body will not have the nature of the flesh. In the flesh, you can do no good thing, produce divine good. The flesh can produce God's good, but only human good, which is abhorrent to God.

7:19 For the good that I will *to do*, I do not do; but the evil I will not *to do*, that I practice.

For the good that I want to do (serve God), I do not do: but the evil I desire not to do, that I do (practice.)

When a believer is carnal, he can only depend on his own energy to control himself. Consequently, his own strength is the flesh which also has him under its control. The two areas of the flesh are the area of strength, (human good) and the area of weakness (sins). The carnal believer sins from the flesh then tries to control himself with good deeds from the flesh. He may do good for awhile, but he cannot maintain it. The carnal believer has the Holy Spirit living in him, but the Spirit does not control him. The only thing the carnal believer can habitually do, is produce human good or commit sins.

7:20 Now if I do what I will not *to do*, it is no longer I who do it, but sin that dwells in me.

Here, Paul admits that he has lost control and is under the thumb of sin, the flesh.

7:21 ¶ I find then a law, that evil is present with me, the one who wills to do good.

Laws always work and are never removed. They have to be overridden by a greater law. This law of the flesh has to be overridden by the law of the Spirit (Romans 8).

7:22 For I delight in the law of God according to the inward man.

The inward man is the human spirit, indwelled by the Holy Spirit. The Spirit is always willing to follow God, but the flesh is weak.

7:23 But I see another law in my members, warring against the law of my mind, and bringing me into captivity to the law of sin which is in my members.

The opposing law to the spirit and indwelling Holy Spirit, is the nature of the flesh which lives in our bodies, our human members. Both the human spirit and the flesh are warring for control of the soul, the mind. The mind is the swing vote. If the mind is controlled by the spirit, the person is spiritual. If the mind if controlled by the flesh, the person is carnal.

7:24 O wretched man that I am! Who will deliver me from this body of death?

Paul has now recognized the problem, he is carnal and under the control of the flesh, sin. He has found that living the Christian life by his own strength is impossible.

7:25 I thank God—through Jesus Christ our Lord! ¶ So then, with the mind I myself serve the law of God, but with the flesh the law of sin.

Paul has also seen the power of the decision of his soul. When he decides to follow his flesh, he is carnal. When he decides to follow his spirit, he is spiritual. From his soul, if he acknowledges his sinful acts, he is forgiven. He then decides to follow the word and his human spirit and he is spiritual. In Romans 8 Paul will find the greater law of the spirit of life in Christ Jesus.

8:1–39 Deliverance and Freedom

We have seen in the previous chapter that we were at one time married to the flesh and now to our new nature (2 Corinthians 5:17). The first marriage had a counselor, the law. The new marriage has a counselor, the indwelling Holy Spirit. There were children with each marriage. The first produced two children, human good and sin (good and evil). The second produces divine good and righteousness. Chapter 7 of Romans deals with deliverance from the previous husband and freedom with the new.

I. Experiential Sanctification (1–17)

Verse 1 teaches positional sanctification must always precede experiential sanctification.

8:1 ¶ There is therefore now no condemnation to those who are in Christ Jesus,[a] who do not walk according to the flesh, but according to the Spirit.

There is therefore now no condemnation (judgment) to those who are in Christ Jesus (who walk not after the flesh, but after to the Spirit is not found in original text in verse 1, but found in verse 4).

A. Points on Positional Sanctification

1. 1 Corinthians 12:13 is the means of sanctification: baptism into the Body of Christ.

2. Characteristics of Sanctification.

   a) Not an emotional experience.

   b) Not progressive.

   c) Not related to human merit.

   d) Eternal. Will not be changed by God or man.

   e) Experience is known only by scripture.

3. Results are found in Ephesians 1:3-6.

4. This brings newness of life (2 Corinthians 5:17).

5. Security of our sanctification is found (Romans 8:38,39).

Verses 2-4, teaches true spirituality. Verse 2 teaches us about settling the great conflict between the two laws.

8:2 For the law of the Spirit of life in Christ Jesus has made me free from the law of sin and death.

The only place you can have the Spirit which produces life is in Christ. You must be born again to have the Holy Spirit. The sin nature (flesh) produces death. Paul is saying, "I have been made free from the law of the sin nature which produced death."

B. Points on the Law of Spirituality

1. Every believer is indwelled by the Spirit (1 Corinthians 3:16, Romans 8:10, Colossians 1:27).

2. Every believer is commanded to be filled with the Holy Spirit (Luke 24:49, Acts 1:4,8, Ephesians 5:18).

3. Every believer is commanded to be led and walk by means of the Spirit (Galatians 5:16, Romans 13:14).

4. A believer out of fellowship has quenched the Spirit and is called carnal (1 Corinthians 3:1-3, 1 John 1:6, 1 Thessalonians 5:19).

5. The believer filled with the Spirit and walking by means of the Spirit, is not subject to the sin nature (Romans 8:2, 10:4, Galatians 5:18,23).

6. The believer controlled by the Spirit fulfills two main objectives.

    a) Glorifies Jesus Christ (John 7:39, 16:14, 1Corinthians 6:19,20, Philippians 1:20).

    b) Fulfills the law (Romans 8:2-4).

7. The believer who follows and is controlled by the Holy Spirit, imitates God (Ephesians 5:1,18). The believer who is not controlled by the Spirit imitates the unbeliever (1 Corinthians 3:3, Galatians 5:19-21, Ephesians 5:7,14).

8. The believer controlled by the Holy Spirit has production acceptable to God and Jesus Christ.

9. The believer who is not controlled by the Holy Spirit imitates the unbeliever (1 Corinthians 3:3, Galatians 5:19-21, Ephesians 5:7,14).

10. The believer controlled by the Holy Spirit has production acceptable to God (Ephesians 2:10).

C. Points on the Law of Carnality

1. The believer continues to possess the nature of the flesh (sin), or

the ability to sin, after salvation (Romans 7:21, Galatians 5:19, 1 John 1:8).

2. This nature is desperately wicked (Jeremiah 17:9, Romans 7:18).

3. This nature has many facets and two trends:

   a) Asceticism: religious good deeds, human morality.

   b) Lasciviousness: sins, immorality.

4. This nature is passed on in mankind through physical birth (Psalm 51:5, Romans 5:12, 1 Timothy 2:13,14).

5. The believer being controlled by the flesh is called carnal (Romans 7:14, 1 Corinthians 3:1-3).

6. The flesh frustrates our production in life (Romans 7:15, Galatians 2:21).

7. This nature is not found in the resurrection body of the believer (Philippians 3:21, 1 John 3:1-3).

8. This nature has many names in the word of God.

   a) Flesh (Galatians 5:16).

   b) Old Man (Ephesians 4:22, Colossians 3:9).

   c) Carnal (Romans 7:14, 1 Corinthians 3:3).

   d) Sin (Romans 5:12, 7:14, 1 John 1:8).

   e) Heart of Man (Jeremiah 17:9, Matthew 15:19).

8:3 For what the law could not do in that it was weak through the flesh, God *did* by sending His own Son in the likeness of sinful flesh, on account of sin: He condemned sin in the flesh,

This verse introduces us to the third law, the Mosaic. First was the Spirit of life. Second was sin and death. The weakness of the law is that it tried to produce life from the outside in. But since the sin nature exists in our flesh, the law simply excited this and continued producing spiritual death. God, once and for all, sent His own Son in the likeness of sinful flesh. Jesus did not have sinful flesh, but was sent by His Father into the earth with a body that looked like everyone else's.

When Jesus went to the cross, He condemned the sin nature and thus removed the condemnation of all personal sin. He conquered sin at its roots. He removed the penalty of the source of sin and thus any manifestation of its acts. "Behold the Lamb of God (Jesus) which takes away the sin (nature) of the world" (John 1:29).

8:4 that the righteous requirement of the law might be fulfilled in us who do not walk according to the flesh but according to the Spirit.

That (in order that) the righteousness (requirements) of the law might (subjunctive mood: potential) be fulfilled in us who do not walk according to the flesh but according to the Spirit.

This is the fulfillment of the law of Moses, or living by the law of the Spirit of life. Only in fellowship with the Lord can the law be fulfilled in us. We are the righteousness of the law (v. 1), but as we remain in fellowship and walk according to the leading of the Holy Spirit, we fulfill the righteousness which is in us and in the law. Again, this is potential, our choice to walk in the control of the Holy Spirit.

D. Walking
Let's look a little more closely at walking.

1. Walking denotes an outward function which parallels a spiritual function.

2. Walking denotes a function of the believer in the life of faith.

3. Walking is compatible with one day at a time (Matthew 6:34), just as walking requires one step at a time.

4. No one gets from one place to another in one step. Spiritual maturity requires many steps (daily faith in the word of God) from babyhood to adult.

5. Walking requires many things (eating, breathing, looking, thinking). Yet we never consider these things, we just walk. Our spiritual walk is a result of our spiritual relationship with the Lord and intake of the word of God.

6. Spheres in the believers walk.

   a) Word (3 John 3)

   b) Holy Spirit (Romans 8:4, Galatians 5:16).

   c) Faith (2 Corinthians 5:7).

   d) Love (Ephesians 5:2).

   e) Honesty (Romans 13:13).

    f) Good works (Ephesians 2:10).

    g) The worth of our vocation (Ephesians 4:1).

    h) In the light of fellowship (1 John 1:7).

7. Walking is a description of progress, growth and maintaining fellowship with God.

8:5 For those who live according to the flesh set their minds on the things of the flesh, but those *who live* according to the Spirit, the things of the Spirit.

For they that are after (walk according to) the flesh (carnal) do mind (set their minds on or think after) the things of the flesh; but they that live after (according to) the Spirit, the things of the Spirit.

We are what we think. We become carnal through our thoughts. Our soul becomes carnal, never our spirit. We are to think on the word and remain spiritual (Philippians 4:8, 2 Corinthians 10:5, Isaiah 26:3).

8:6 For to be carnally minded *is* death, but to be spiritually minded *is* life and peace.

This is temporal death, not positional death. This is the type of death the prodigal was said to have (Luke 15:24) while he was in carnality. Peace also is a fruit of the Holy Spirit and recreated human spirit. Out of fellowship, you cannot produce the fruit of the Spirit (1 John 1:6-8).

E. Seven Types of Death in the Word

1. Physical Death (Philippians 1:21, 2 Corinthians 5:8, Matthew 8:22).

2. Spiritual Death (Ephesians 2:1, Romans 6:23).

3. Second Death (unbeliever at last judgment)-(Hebrews 9:27, Revelation 20:12).

4. Positional Death (Romans 6:2-4, Colossians 2:12, 3:4).

5. Operational Death (Christian production) (James 2:26).

6. Sexual Death (no longer able to have children) (Romans 4:17-21, Hebrews 11:11).

7. Temporal Death (carnal believer, out of fellowship) (Romans 8:6,13, Luke 15:24,32, James 1:15, Revelation 3:1).

8:7 Because the carnal mind *is* enmity against God; for it is not subject to the law of God, nor indeed can be.

Because the carnal mind is enmity against (the enemy of) God; for it is not subject (under orders) to the law of God, neither indeed can be (it is not able).

The Holy Spirit lives in your human spirit. When your mind is carnal, you have a war in your inner man. The mind becomes an enemy to your spirit.

8:8 So then, those who are in the flesh cannot please God.

F. In or Out of Fellowship

1. In fellowship with God
    a) Law of righteousness is fulfilled (v. 4)
    b) You mind the things of the Spirit (v. 5)
    c) You have life and peace (v. 6)
    d) You are a friend of God (v. 7)
    e) You can please God (v. 8)

2. Out of fellowship with God:
    a) Righteousness of the law is unfulfilled (v. 4)
    b) You mind the things of the flesh (v. 5)
    c) You have temporal death (v. 6)
    d) You are the enemy of God (v. 7)
    e) You cannot please God (v. 8)

8:9 ¶ But you are not in the flesh but in the Spirit, if indeed the Spirit of God dwells in you. Now if anyone does not have the Spirit of Christ, he is not His.

Paul again reminds them he is addressing them as believers and not unbelievers. The power of the flesh was conquered in them the moment they were born again. They have the potential to walk pleasing to God and have since the moment of salvation. They have the power in them to please God, the power of the Holy Spirit. If the Holy Spirit does not live in a person, he is not a Christian and he does not belong to Jesus Christ. Acting righteous is not difficult when you are righteous.

G. More on Two Husbands
Verse 10 amplifies the two husbands spoken of chapter 7.

8:10 And if Christ *is* in you, the body *is* dead because of sin, but the Spirit *is* life because of righteousness.

The two husbands are defined as our body (first husband) and the Holy Spirit (second husband).

8:11 But if the Spirit of Him who raised Jesus from the dead dwells in you, He who raised Christ from the dead will also give life to your mortal bodies through His Spirit who dwells in you.

The Holy Spirit in us gives life to our bodies. Even though the body has the nature of the flesh, it can be controlled from the inside out and can produce the righteousness of the law.

8:12 ¶ Therefore, brethren, we are debtors—not to the flesh, to live according to the flesh.

This is our second death taught in Romans. The first was 1:15 to give the gospel to the world.

8:13 For if you live according to the flesh you will die; but if by the Spirit you put to death the deeds of the body, you will live.

For if you live after (according to) the flesh you will die (temporal death); but if you through the Spirit do mortify (put to death) the deeds of the body, you shall live (temporal life).

When we are controlled by the flesh, we produce temporal death, or things which have no lasting value. But when we follow the Holy Spirit, and we are in fellowship with the Lord we produce spiritual things which have eternal life and produce reward in time and eternity.

8:14 For as many as are led by the Spirit of God, these are sons of God.

You cannot be led by the Spirit when you are carnal. You are then led by the flesh and its lusts. You can only be led by the Spirit when you are in fellowship, spiritual. You are also greatly hampered in being led by the Spirit until you know the word. You cannot do God's will until you know His will. Hearing which produces faith, comes before doing.

8:15 For you did not receive the spirit of bondage again to fear, but you received the Spirit of adoption by whom we cry out, "Abba, Father."

For you have not received the spirit of bondage again to (leading to) fear, but you received the Spirit of adoption (sonship) whereby we cry, Abba, Father.

Under the new covenant, with the Holy Spirit living in us, we no longer see God as only God, but as our Father, and we are children in His family. *Abba* is Aramaic (Chaldean and Hebrew) for father. Abraham's name is *Ab* (father) *raham* (of many nations).

8:16 The Spirit Himself bears witness with our spirit that we are children of God,

The Spirit Himself bears witness (supports by testimony, confirming) with our spirit that we are the children of God:

The way the Spirit confirms our sonship is by impressing the word to our soul. In verse 14 we are said to be mature sons when we are led by the Spirit. In verse 16 the Spirit lets us know through the word we are children.
    H. Heirship

8:17 and if children, then heirs—heirs of God and joint heirs with Christ, if indeed we suffer with *Him*, that we may also be glorified together.

Heirship is based on birth, not works. No one is an heir because they are born an heir. We also are not heirs based of ourselves, but because of who we are in. We are an heir because we share the heirship of Jesus. We are heirs with God through joint heirship with the Son.
Let's look at little more closely at heirship.

1. Christ is the creator of all things (Colossians 1:16,17, Hebrews 1:2,10, Revelation 4:11).

2. Christ is the heir of all things (Colossians 1:18, Hebrews 1:2).

3. Heirship is based on sonship (Romans 8:16,17, Galatians 4:7).

4. Salvation makes us an heir of God through joint-heirship with Christ (Romans 8:17, Ephesians 1:11, Colossians 1:12).

5. Heirship demands eternal life (1 Corinthians 15:50, Titus 3:7).

6. Heirship is based on election (Hebrews 9:15).

7. The inheritance is eternal (1 Peter 1:4).

   a) Incorruptible: cannot be destroyed by death.

   b) Undefiled: cannot be contaminated by the flesh.

   c) Fades not away: cannot be destroyed by catastrophe Satan or man.

   d) Reserved: cannot be destroyed by time.

8. Heirship is based on grace. It is all the work of Jesus Christ (Galatians 3:18).

9. Unbelievers do not have an inheritance (1 Corinthians 6:9,10, Galatians 5:21).

10. The Holy Spirit is the down payment on our inheritance (Ephesians 1:14, Galatians 4:6).

II. Experiential Suffering (18–39)

Teaching on suffering begins in verse 18: How a mature believer handles suffering and the benefits of the maturity which can come through suffering .

8:18 ⸓ For I consider that the sufferings of this present time are not worthy *to be compared* with the glory which shall be revealed in us.

For I reckon (consider, calculate, come to a conclusion) that the sufferings of this present time are not worthy to be compared with the glory which shall be revealed in us.

Whatever we suffer in life is not even worthy to be mentioned in comparison to what heaven will be like. Paul states in 2 Corinthians 4:17 that the afflictions of this life are a light weight and the glory of eternity with Christ is a far exceeding and eternal weight. The two can never be compared.

8:19 For the earnest expectation of the creation eagerly waits for the revealing of the sons of God

Nature is saying the same thing Paul is saying. Nature is also awaiting the return of Jesus to release the earth from bondage. Nature is not waiting for the sons of God, but the manifestation, the revealing of them. This is not the Rapture of the Church, but the second coming, the return of Jesus to rule over the earth (Revelation 19:11-16). It will occur at the end of the tribulation and usher in the millennium. The Church will return in resurrection bodies, with Jesus on that day.

8:20 For the creation was subjected to futility, not willingly, but because of Him who subjected *it* in hope;

For the creature (creation) was made subjected to vanity (futility, darkness, emptiness) not willingly, but by reason (because) of Him (Christ) who has subjected the same in hope,

Nature was made subject (servant) to vanity in Genesis 3 when the curse of Adam's disobedience was placed on the earth. God allowed the curse to come because He told Adam it would come if he disobeyed God. God allowed the curse knowing the remedy would come through the cross. God did this in hope for the future. God gave Adam and Eve glory, honor and dominion. Now because of the curse, man can only produce cursed offspring. Satan's entire kingdom is cursed. When the creature decides to be born again, he moves out of Satan's kingdom and back into God's. He has life again.

8:21 because the creation itself also will be delivered from the bondage of corruption into the glorious liberty of the children of God.

Nature will be delivered from the bondage of corruption at the start of the millennium. No more thorns, storms, war, etc. Nature will be delivered into liberty at the same time the children of God return with Jesus to rule the earth. The Church's deliverance came seven years earlier at the Rapture.

A. Three Groans (or Sufferings)

1. The first of three groans mentioned in chapter 8 (v. 22).

8:22 For we know that the whole creation groans and labors with birth pangs together until now.

For we know that the whole creation groans and travails (labors) in pain (with birth pangs) together until now.

Verse 18 tells us the sufferings (groanings) now are not to be compared to the glory yet to be revealed. Groanings look back to the fall of Adam when sin was conceived. Travail looks forward to the second advent when deliverance is come and the curse removed. At the time of writing, nature was groaning and travailing. It is more intense today. Every time we see sin and its effects around it causes two things, groanings and travail. We are angry at Satan but we rejoice in hope of the day of deliverance.

2. The Second Groan (v. 23).

8:23 Not only *that*, but we also who have the firstfruits of the Spirit, even we ourselves groan within ourselves, eagerly waiting for the adoption, the redemption of our body.

Even believers suffer. The part of us which is tied in with nature, our bodies, still maintain the curse. We have the nature of the flesh which has been the object of discussion for quite a few chapters. When nature groans, we groan also. Trials not only come to the sinner, but to those who have been born again. Those who are born again are not exempt but contrariwise are more of a target than ever for Satan. The adoption, mentioned here, is yet to come. Adoption has three uses in the word. Spirit: adopted at birth, soul: adopted at spiritual maturity and body: adopted at the Rapture. Our body, which has the nature of the flesh, sin, has yet to be redeemed, or adopted. This will occur when we receive a resurrection body.

8:24 For we were saved in this hope, but hope that is seen is not hope; for why does one still hope for what he sees?

Hope is always future. Hope of the return of Jesus gives us comfort. Salvation is past, present and future. Our spirit has already been born again. Our souls are being renewed day by day. And our body is facing redemption in the future. This verse is teaching the same thing as Hebrews 11:1: "faith is the substance of things hoped for." Faith and hope work together to obtain what cannot be seen. But once it arrives it no longer has to be seen by faith. It has been manifested and can be seen with the eyes. Paul is saying, there is a salvation, deliverance, attached to hope. One form of daily comfort, is to realize Jesus is coming soon for us to redeem our cursed bodies. Also, this cursed world will be redeemed one day when Jesus returns to set up His eternal kingdom. On that day, the kingdoms of this world will become the kingdoms of our Lord and of His Christ, and He shall reign forever and ever (Revelation 11:15).

8:25 But if we hope for what we do not see, we eagerly wait for *it* with perseverance.

Patience and hope are two cooperating powers which work with faith. We do not yet see the millennial reign of Jesus, nor our resurrection bodies. But we know by faith in God's word that it is coming. Hope is the picture before us and faith working with patience will get us there.

3. The Final Groan (v. 26-27).

8:26 ¶ Likewise the Spirit also helps in our weaknesses. For we do not know what we should pray for as we ought, but the Spirit Himself makes intercession for us with groanings which cannot be uttered.

We have had help from the word, producing faith, hope and patience. Now, we have help from the Holy Spirit. The infirmity the Holy Spirit helps us with is our ignorance of how to pray in certain situations. In verse 22 Paul said "we know." In verse 28 Paul will say again, "we know." In between, in verse 26, we have a "we know not." In certain situations of life we know the scripture which applies to the problem. In other situations we have no idea how to pray. The Holy Spirit is there to help us and give us wisdom. He does this in the midst of our groanings with words which cannot be spoken in our natural, earthly language. This is a reference to the power of praying in the Spirit, praying in tongues.

8:27 Now He who searches the hearts knows what the mind of the Spirit *is*, because He makes intercession for the saints according to *the will of* God.

Because the Holy Spirit knows the plan of God and the thinking of Jesus, He can transfer that wisdom to our heart since He lives there. This comes to our heart by praying in the Holy Spirit, in tongues. Our sensitivity to the Holy Spirit increases as we pray in tongues. We can hear the Spirit's voice and leading and pray in line with God's will.

8:28 ¶ And we know that all things work together for good to those who love God, to those who are the called according to *His* purpose.

And we know (perfect tense) that all things work together (*sunergeo*: co-operate, assist with each other) for good (*agathos*: divine, eternal good) to them that love God, to them who are the called according to His purpose.

This refers to all things we face in life, whether good or bad, blessings or trials. It does not say all things are good, although some things we face are good. Each day we have a certain amount of good and bad. But our spiritual lives are not determined by our circumstances. We must rely on the word of God in us. Everything in life has its place, even suffering. Although God does not send suffering, Satan and the fallen world does. Suffering helps us to understand where we stand in life. Suffering puts us under pressure and reveals what is in us. God gives us the weapons to handle the problems which are always superior to Satan's temptations and traps. So, it is not the trials which makes us strong, but the faith we use in the trials which strengthens us. No matter the problem, God has a way of escape planned and all things, good and bad, will work together, cooperate with each other, for our good. All ingredients, good tasting or bad, will work together and come out of the oven as a chocolate cake. Only the believer who knows and uses the word of God can make all things work together for his good. Those are the ones who love God and keep His commandments (John 14:15). Romans 8:28 is for the believer who qualifies in two areas:

1. They are elect-born again.

2. They love God-mature.

8:29 For whom He foreknew, He also predestined *to be* conformed to the image of His Son, that He might be the firstborn among many brethren.

For whom He did foreknow (*proginoskoto*: know ahead of time), He also predestined (*proorizo*: to predesign) to be conformed to the image of His Son, that He might be the firstborn among many brethren.

Predestination is built on the foundation of God's omniscience, His foreknowledge. "Whom God knew ahead of time would be saved, He predesigned a plan for their life" (see 1 Peter 1:2). Predestination is only for believers not unbelievers. Predestination is not just to be born again, but to be changed into the very image of Jesus Christ. This means God's purpose for us in life is to grow up and be like Jesus in every area of our life; disciples, not just converts. Jesus became the firstborn in God's family among

many who would be born again later.
The firstborn of Israel had three rights:

1. Rulership

2. Priesthood

3. Double Portion

We become joint (equal) heirs with Him and we share all these rights with Him.

8:30 Moreover whom He predestined, these He also called; whom He called, these He also justified; and whom He justified, these He also glorified.

Moreover whom He predestined, them He also called (elected); whom He called, them He also justified (imputed righteousness); and whom He justified, them He also glorified.

Only believers are elected based on their choice to receive Jesus as Savior. Sinners are never elected to suffer in hell and eventually the lake of fire. Election for believers is God's choice. The lake of fire is the unbeliever's choice. This verse is all positional truth. We are elected, predestined, justified and glorified spiritually.

Glorification is mentioned at the end of this verse. It, along with the other blessings mentioned, is past tense. Before the foundation of the world, God saw our choice for salvation, and gave us at that point, a plan for life, made us part of the elect, gave us a call, justified us and glorified us. At this point, most all of those are behind each one of us and we are living in them now. Yet, glorification, a resurrection body, is yet to come, yet seen as already done. If God already sees us in a resurrection body and we have not yet arrived there, then we must be going to make it through the trials we are now experiencing. We must also make it through the next trial and the next until we are raptured out of this world. Heaven, eternity, and a resurrection for us are a sure thing with God.

B. Questions of Suffering

1. First Question: What are the sufferings of this life?

8:31 ¶ What then shall we say to these things? If God *is* for us, who *can be* against us?

The problems and adversities of the Christian life come from Satan and the curse he brought into the earth, the world's system and our own flesh nature. What is the world, the flesh or the devil next to God? Our problems next to us seem big. Our problems next to God are small.

   2. Second Question: If the Father did the hardest thing He ever did when He gave us eternal life, why can't He provide for our problems in life which are much simpler?

8:32 He who did not spare His own Son, but delivered Him up for us all, how shall He not with Him also freely give us all things?

The important teaching of the word of God is not the life of Jesus, but His death and resurrection. Through them, we have eternal life and earthly life more abundantly. Salvation is free and so is everything for this life on earth. Now that we are joined to Him, Grace still gives with no strings attached.

   3. Third Question: Who is the one who comes against us?

8:33 Who shall bring a charge against God's elect? *It is* God who justifies.

It is Satan who brings charges against us in heaven (Zechariah 3:1, Revelation 12:10), but it is God who justifies us and Jesus who defends us (1 John 2:1). God is not our condemner.

   4. Fourth Question: Who condemns us?

8:34 Who *is* he who condemns? *It is* Christ who died, and furthermore is also risen, who is even at the right hand of God, who also makes intercession for us.

The opposition of people, believers and unbelievers, who condemn us. Our true enemy is Satan and our deliverer is God. This verse says, who has the right to judge? To judge you must be in a position to do so. Judges sit in high places. Only one person has the right to spiritual judgment, Jesus Christ. He purchased that right through death, burial, resurrection, ascension and seating at the right hand of God.

   5. Fifth Question: Who can separate us from Christ?

8:35 Who shall separate us from the love of Christ? *Shall*

tribulation, or distress, or persecution, or famine, or nakedness, or peril, or sword?

Who shall separate us from the love of Christ? Shall tribulation (extreme
pressure), or distress (anguish or worry), or persecution (pressure from
unbelievers), or famine (lack of food), or nakedness (lack of clothing), or
peril (life threatening situations), or sword (war)?

Look at salvation from the Father's eyes of love. There is not one believer
the Father does not love. Seven things are mentioned in this verse which
are extreme to us but cannot separate us from God's love. God's love is
bigger than anything we can imagine. We think of deliverance in peril,
food in famine, clothing in times of nakedness. But God never forgets us.
He is asking us to think of His faithfulness and His word in every situation
we face. The answer to our problems will be delivered to us in due time.

**8:36 As it is written: "For Your sake we are killed all day long;
We are accounted as sheep for the slaughter."**

As it is written (in Psalm 44:22), For Your sake we are killed (seen as dead)
all day long; We are accounted (calculated) as sheep for the slaughter.

We are in danger all day from unseen forces because we are believers
and have His life and nature. We are always enemies to Satan. We are not
sheep for the slaughter, but accounted, viewed or seen, as sheep to be
killed and eaten. This is seen from the viewpoint of the wolf (Satan). He
looks at us as prey, easily taken. But when our defense is the word we are
protected from him. Our protection is the love of the Shepherd.

**8:37 ¶ Yet in all these things we are more than conquerors
through Him who loved us.**

Jesus Christ is our personal strength through the Holy Spirit and the word
of God. We are greater than Satan, demons, unbelievers, carnal Christians
or the problems of life through Jesus Christ who loves us.

F. Ten Things That Cannot Separate Us from God's Love

**8:38 For I am persuaded that neither death nor life, nor angels
nor principalities nor powers, nor things present nor things
to come,**

1. Physical death cannot separate us from God's love. In fact, it puts us into His presence (2 Corinthians 5:8).

2. This life has nothing which can separate us from God's love. No person, sin, experience or place is more powerful than the love of Jesus Christ to keep us.

3. No elect or fallen angel, including Satan himself, can separate us from God's love.

4. No principalities, demons of any rank, can destroy us or separate us from God's love.

5. The powers that be, human governments or rulers, cannot separate us from God's love and keeping power.

6. The present age we live in, the Church Age, has nothing we need to fear. Each day is a time of faith and joy as we anticipate God's plan of success for this life and eternity.

7. Things to come after death have no power to remove God's love from our life. The Judgment Seat Of Christ, Second Advent, destruction of earth and the final judgment of sinners, fallen angels, demons, religion and Satan himself will all take place without removing us from the love of Jesus Christ.

8:39 nor height nor depth, nor any other created thing, shall be able to separate us from the love of God which is in Christ Jesus our Lord.

8. Height, the highest mountain or tallest building should bring no fear to us. Nature or the inventions of man are no match for the love of our Savior.

9. We also cannot go to the lowest depth of the earth or ocean and escape the love and presence of God (Psalm 139:7-10).

10. Anything in creation, visible or invisible, made by God, Satan or man will ever be able to separate us from the love of God which is in Christ Jesus our Lord.

9:1–33 Israel and Grace

Chapter 9 of Romans begins a three-chapter parenthesis explaining how Israel fits into the grace picture, and the coexistence of human and divine will on the earth.

1. In heaven, only God's will is done.

2. On earth there are three wills being done.

    a. God's will through believers

    b. Satan's will through believers and unbelievers

    c. Man's will

3. The first time man's will comes in line with God's will is at salvation.

4. From the time of salvation on, how the believer's will lines up with God's will is through obedience to the word of God. His word is His will.

I. Israel (1–11)

A. Paul's Deep Love for the Jewish Nation
He begins with a triple oath in verse one.

> **9:1 ¶ I tell the truth in Christ, I am not lying, my conscience also bearing me witness in the Holy Spirit,**

Paul's conscience bore witness based on what he knew from the word of God. In chapter 9, Paul is concerned about the Jews because he is one by birth (Philippians 3:4-6). But, a true Jew is one who has the lineage of Abraham, Isaac and Jacob and is born again. "Not all Israel is Israel" will be taught in v. 6. Within the nation of Israel is "the commonwealth of Israel," or believing Jews (Ephesians 2:12).

> **9:2 that I have great sorrow and continual grief in my heart.**

Paul's love for Israel leaves him in pain each day for their rejection of Jesus as Savior and Messiah.

> **9:3 For I could wish that I myself were accursed from Christ for my brethren, my countrymen[a] according to the flesh,**

The nation of Israel is under a curse today (Romans 11:25) and are blinded from the reality of Jesus Christ. They will be under the curse until the Rapture. As individuals they can come out from the curse by faith in Jesus Christ.

B. Eight Areas of Blessing for Jews

The blessings given here are strictly for the Jewish nation. All of them teach of Jesus' redemption.

9:4 who are Israelites, to whom *pertain* the adoption, the glory, the covenants, the giving of the law, the service *of God*, and the promises;

1. The adoption: This refers to the firstborn of God (Exodus 4:22, Jeremiah 31:9). The firstborn was the first one adopted. This gave all rights and privileges of the father. These privileges may be temporarily suspended but will resume and be fulfilled at the Second Advent of Jesus (Isaiah 66:22).

2. The glory: This is the shekinah glory, the cloud of God's presence in the Holy of Holies (Exodus 24:16, Ezekiel 1:28).

3. The covenants: This is plural. There were four unconditional covenants given to Israel. The first two have been given and fulfilled. The next two will be fulfilled at the second advent of Jesus.

   a) Abrahamic

   b) Davidic

   c) Palestinian

   d) New

4. The giving of the law: The law was given to Israel only (Exodus 19:3, Leviticus 26:46, Romans 3:19). The law was not given to Gentiles (Deuteronomy 4:8) and not to the church (Acts 15:5,24, Romans 6:14, Galatians 2:19, 5:18,23).

5. The service of God: The ritual of the priesthood in worship and service.

6. The promises: There are three categories of promises.

   a) Messianic: God promised the Jews first a Messiah. He came first to "the lost sheep of the house of Israel" (Matthew 10:6). After their rejection He turned to the Gentiles.

   b) Comfort: Promises for times of persecution and trouble.

c) Future: Second advent and millennium. These were promised to the Jew for the possession of the land and fulfillment of the four covenants.

9:5 of whom *are* the fathers and from whom, according to the flesh, Christ *came*, who is over all, *the* eternally blessed God. Amen.

Verse 5 continues the eight monopolies of the Jewish people.

7. Of whom are the fathers: The Jewish fathers were men of faith. Abraham, Isaac and Jacob were taught faith principles and passed them to their children.

8. From whom Christ came: The Jewish nation was the one chosen to bring in the Messiah to the world. Jesus was a Jew in His humanity.

9:6 ¶ But it is not that the word of God has taken no effect. For they *are* not all Israel who *are* of Israel,

Yet, there were many Jews saved in the Old Testament. The Word preached in faith will produce results in the hearts of the people looking for redemption. Not all racial Jews are the true Israel. Those Jews who have received Jesus as their savior are the true Jews. The Jews at the time of this writing were blaming God for all their troubles. Instead of correcting their unbelief, they looked for someone else to blame, a scapegoat, and they put the blame on God.

7. They were promised all the land of Palestine and as yet, they never dwelled there. "It's all God's fault."

8. They were promised a Messiah who would rule forever on the throne of David. He has never sat on the throne in Jerusalem. "It's all God's fault."

Chapter 9 deals with God's faithfulness even though man is unfaithful. All these promises will come to pass despite the attitude of the Jews. The kingdom will come despite Satan, the Jews or all of our unbelief.

C. Not Ishmael, but Isaac

In verse 7, Paul begins to tell of the Jew which will receive the promises. Those who are of faith are the true Israel; not Ishmael, but Isaac; not Esau, but Jacob.

9:7 nor *are they* all children because they are the seed of

Abraham; but, "In Isaac your seed shall be called."

Natural Jews were not what God was looking for. Neither is He looking for natural people of any race today. God is looking for people to be born again, made into a spiritual race today as He was looking for in Abraham's day. The natural seed is not what counts with God, but the regenerate, those born again (Matthew 3:9). We are not all children of God, nor are we all brothers and sisters because of anything attached to natural birth, color, race or sex. True equality and relationship can only come through accepting Jesus as Savior and joining God's family. Galatians 3:26 tells us we are all children of God through faith in Jesus Christ. Isaac was the faith seed of promise. Ishmael was the flesh seed by works, self-effort.

9:8 That is, those who *are* the children of the flesh, these *are* not the children of God; but the children of the promise are counted as the seed.

Being born a racial Jew does not give anyone an in with God. Natural birth does not make you a child of God. Ishmael was as much a natural child of Abraham as Isaac. The first birth does not make you a child of God. It takes another birth, the new birth. Ishmael was not rejected because he was born from a bondwoman or even out of wedlock. The following generations show this. Isaac had twin sons born through the wife, one was accepted and one was rejected. Jacob had twelve sons, born through two wives and two servants. All were accepted.

9:9 For this *is* the word of promise: "At this time I will come and Sarah shall have a son."

The promise to Abraham was a son from Sarah. The impatience of Abraham brought about Ishmael.

9:10 ¶ And not only *this*, but when Rebecca also had conceived by one man, *even* by our father Isaac

Isaac (man of faith) is also our father as is Abraham. Ishmael is not called our father because this is the spiritual race being taught, not the natural.

9:11 (for *the children* not yet being born, nor having done any good or evil, that the purpose of God according to election might stand, not of works but of Him who calls),

The children were not yet born, nor had they done any good or evil.

God knew while the children were in the womb that one would reject the Lord and one would accept; one would be a man of faith and the other of self-works. What God saw from the womb was the future of both sons, Jacob and Esau. He saw Jacob would receive Him and Esau would not. This is election by foreknowledge and grace, spiritual predestination, not foreordination.

II. God and His Man (12–33)

A. Foreknowledge-Predestination-Calling-Justification-Glorification

Election and predestination are all based on God's foreknowledge of our will (Romans 8:29-30).

9:12 it was said to her, "The older shall serve the younger."

God's foreknowledge, not foreordination, was made known to Rebecca before their birth.

9:13 As it is written, "Jacob I have loved, but Esau I have hated."

God did not hate Esau, but his unbelief. And, God loved the faith of Jacob (Hebrews 11:6).
Moses and Pharaoh become the subject of verses 14-18 just as Esau and Jacob in verses 10-13.

9:14 ¶ What shall we say then? *Is there* unrighteousness with God? Certainly not!

This is based on verse 13. Does God play favorites or have respect of persons? The answer is NO. God is a respecter of faith. Hate toward anyone concerning birth is sin. Can God sin? God's hatred is not of people, but their ways. Whatever is not of faith is sin. God must judge sin so His mercy toward the righteous can be fulfilled.

9:15 For He says to Moses, "I will have mercy on whomever I will have mercy, and I will have compassion on whomever I will have compassion."

This story is found in Exodus 33:13-23. Moses asked to see the glory of God. God granted Moses' request based on God, not on Moses, God's

mercy, grace and compassion, not Moses' good deeds.
God's mercy and compassion are not based on His sovereignty, but foreknowledge of man's decisions. His compassion and mercy as well as His
hatred is based on man's acceptance of His plan and nothing else.

9:16 So then *it is* not of him who wills, nor of him who runs, but of God who shows mercy.

God's plan of grace for our everyday life is based on our decisions and
God's knowledge ahead of time of our choice. Yet, the plan of redemption
was not put into effect because of our choice, but the sovereignty of God
based on His mercy. Jesus was sent to the cross and still would have died
if no one would have accepted Him.
The ultimate plan of God began with Him and not us. God's compassion
was here before us. The cross is the dividing line of whom God will have a
plan for or not. Yet, He has compassion on all, if they receive Jesus or not.
His compassion provides a plan, but His justice takes over if they reject the
plan. He hates their decision. He does not hate them.

9:17 For the Scripture says to the Pharaoh, "For this very purpose I have raised you up, that I may show My power in you, and that My name may be declared in all the earth."

God did not make Pharaoh rebellious. God saw it in his heart, gave him
plenty of time to repent and change, then used his rebellion to declare His
name through the nations. Through the first plagues, Pharaoh hardened
his own heart (see Exodus 7:22, 8:15, 32, 9:34).
After a point, when it was evident Pharaoh would not repent, God removed all restraints and it was written, "the Lord hardened Pharaoh's
heart" (Exodus 10:1, 20, 27, 11:10, 14:8). There is always mercy before
judgment.
Because of Pharaoh's rebellion toward God, God's reputation was increased in Egypt and Canaan. A large diverse group of races from Egypt
left with the children of Israel. When the spies came to Jericho, Rahab told
them the inhabitants of Canaan had been shaking from the day the children of Israel crossed the Red Sea. That story brought Rahab to a saving
experience with the Lord (Joshua 2:9-11). If anyone opposes God, they will
be the loser (Psalm 7:6-10).

9:18 Therefore He has mercy on whom He wills, and whom He wills He hardens.

God's will is based on our will, our faith or rejection. He has mercy on those who will accept His will and turns from those who reject His will. God does to us what we do to Him. Surely He scorns the scornful, but gives grace to the humble (Proverbs 3:34). God's mercy is based on the cross. We must decide to accept His work or not. This anticipates chapter 10. God's decisions are consistent with His character. His character is righteousness. His righteousness is a perfect standard which either blesses or curses. If we accept Jesus' righteousness for our own, God blesses. If we refuse Jesus' righteousness, we accept our own and do not measure up to God's perfect standard. God has no alternative but to condemn.

B. Potter and Clay

9:19 ¶ You will say to me then, "Why does He still find fault? For who has resisted His will?"

It is not up to us to say, "I have followed the Lord and done nothing wrong. Why have I still turned out this way? God still tells me through His word I have not arrived. I can't seem to please Him. It must be God's fault I am the way I am." No one is the way they are because it's God's fault. Any fault is with us and not Him.

9:20 But indeed, O man, who are you to reply against God? Will the thing formed say to him who formed *it*, "Why have you made me like this?"

Clay moulding is used in two places in the Old Testament: Isaiah 45:8-12 and Jeremiah 18:6-10. We are born as lumps of clay and are molded into vessels of honor as we accept Jesus as our Savior and follow His word into discipleship (2 Timothy 2:20,21). We are the way we are because of our decision to follow. His power shapes us as we submit to His word and Spirit. The glory still goes to Him because of His power and grace, not our faith. So quit asking God "Why have you made me like this?" and say, "I am the way I am because of my obedience to His will. If I want to be better, I need to grow more in His word and faith so I can be a vessel of honor."

9:21 Does not the potter have power over the clay, from the same lump to make one vessel for honor and another for dishonor?

We do not have the ultimate power, God does. Our rebellion toward God does us no good. In the end, He will win and not us. God's desire is to make each of us a vessel of honor. Only He can make us a vessel of honor and only we can allow Him to do so. The clay is man with his free will. The potter is God. A vessel of dishonor can be a believer or unbeliever. The unbeliever rejects the righteousness of God and falls back on his own righteousness. He will eventually face hell and the lake of fire, banishment from the presence of God. The believer rejects the life of faith, living by God's word and faces misery in life and lack of rewards in eternity, even though he will be forever in heaven with God.

In this chapter so far, we have had three vessels of dishonor—Ishmael, Esau and Pharaoh—and three vessels of honor—Isaac, Jacob and Moses. We are introducing chapters 10 and 11. The Gentiles will be vessels of honor and the Jews, vessels of dishonor.

9:22 ¶ *What* if God, wanting to show *His* wrath and to make His power known, endured with much longsuffering the vessels of wrath prepared for destruction,

This is a good description of Pharaoh. God endued with much longsuffering the rejection of Pharaoh. God always approaches us with His love. If we reject He shows us His wrath. Many were saved by hearing God's love, others of His wrath. Pharaoh rejected both.

 When a potter approaches clay, his first touch is gentle (love). If the clay is stiff (rejection of His will) he pushes harder (message of His wrath). If the lump still refuses to be molded, the potter can disregard the lump and throw it away. The potter is greater than the clay.

If a person keeps on rejecting God's message, they will eventually face His judgment. He is greater than their rejection. The harder they push against God, the bigger He becomes. He rises each time they rise against Him. He eventually will win. His victory will be just that much more spectacular.

9:23 and that He might make known the riches of His glory on the vessels of mercy, which He had prepared beforehand for glory,

God's plan for us to be conformed into the image of Jesus Christ began before the foundation of the earth. God's plan for us began in eternity past and will continue into eternity future. His plan is glorious if we will just submit to the Potter.

In verse 24, Paul now comes to us, believers in the New Testament. God's plan for Israel to be used by Him is no different than His will for us today.

9:24 even us whom He called, not of the Jews only, but also of the Gentiles?

We were called before the foundation of the world (Ephesians 1:4). In the Old Testament, God's will was to save Gentiles, just like He saved Jews. Today, God's will to save Gentiles is nothing new.

9:25 ¶ As He says also in Hosea: "I will call them My people, who were not My people, and her beloved, who was not beloved."

A reference to Gentiles. God called Gentiles His own people and beloved before this actually came to pass in the Church Age. Although God saved Gentiles in the Old Testament, they were never a part of His center of activity to accomplish His will of evangelism and discipleship. This was for the Jews. After Pentecost, it is the Church, made up of Gentile nations He is using for His plan of evangelism and discipleship.

9:26 "And it shall come to pass in the place where it was said to them, 'You are not My people,' There they shall be called sons of the living God."

Gentiles today who are born again, not only are saved, but also become God's own children, members of the royal family.

9:27 ¶ Isaiah also cries out concerning Israel: "Though the number of the children of Israel be as the sand of the sea, The remnant will be saved.

Although there were many Jews in the land of Palestine and throughout the world in the Old Testament, only a portion of them found the true means of salvation, faith.

9:28 For He will finish the work and cut it short in righteousness, because the Lord will make a short work upon the earth."

The NAS translates this verse:"For The Lord will execute His word upon the earth, thoroughly and quickly."

9:29 ¶ And as Isaiah said before: "Unless the Lord of Sabaoth

had left us a seed, we would have become like Sodom, and we would have been made like Gomorrah."

The seed (remnant of saved Jews in the land at the time) were what preserved the land of Palestine and kept it from the wrath of God as it was in Sodom and Gomorrah. Believers have always been the salt (preserver) of the earth, the land they live in.

9:30 ⁋ What shall we say then? That Gentiles, who did not pursue righteousness, have attained to righteousness, even the righteousness of faith;

What is the conclusion of the argument? The Gentiles of the Old Testament (who did not pursue after God's righteousness) have found it by faith, faith in Jesus Christ. They did not seek righteousness through the law because they were not given the law and did not have the law. They not only have found righteousness, they have traded places with Israel as the custodians of God's message of evangelism and power of the word.

9:31 but Israel, pursuing the law of righteousness, has not attained to the law of righteousness.

Israel pursued righteousness by the law and never attained to righteousness by the law. The law contains righteousness, but it can only be found and kept by a righteous person. But, "there is none righteous, no not one." Only a righteous person can accomplish the righteousness in the law. Righteousness is found by faith in Jesus Christ and the righteousness in the law can only be fulfilled by walking in the Spirit.

9:32 Why? Because *they did* not seek *it* by faith, but as it were, by the works of the law. For they stumbled at that stumbling stone.

The law was never designed to save. It was given for two reasons: expose the problem and reveal the answer to the problem. The problem is sin, the nature of the flesh, and the answer to the problem is faith in Jesus Christ. By searching for redemption by the law, they kept stumbling over the stumbling stone.

9:33 As it is written: "Behold, I lay in Zion a stumbling stone and rock of offense, And whoever believes on Him will not be put to shame."

Jesus Christ is the stumbling stone. He was a stumbling stone to the Jews first because He did not come as a great deliverer, king or prince. He was lowly and not desirable. Salvation has always been the same. Believe on the Lord Jesus Christ (Acts 16:31) whether Old Testament or New.

10:1–21 Israel During the Church Age

Romans 10 is a continuation of Romans 9, and explains God's plan for Israel during the Church Age.

Previously we were told of the failure of the Jews because they tried to attain righteousness by keeping the law. Romans 10 tells us that salvation was closer to the Jew than he imagined. He was looking at ritual, sacrifices and observances of laws for salvation and it was with him all the time, in his heart and mouth. Romans 10 also introduces Romans 11.

I. Six Points of Introduction to Romans 10

A. Uses a Previous Dispensation

1. Gentiles: One race, language, Adam to Babel.

2. Jews: Abraham to the cross, many races and languages.

In the previous dispensation, Israel was responsible to spread the gospel. They failed and spread the law as the means of salvation. They taught salvation as something outward when it was in them all the time. The heart and mouth is the answer, which is in all men, not just Jews.

B. Faith Not Birth

The foundation of Israel is not physical birth, but faith. It is a supernatural race. Abraham was a Gentile, faith made him a Jew. The same with Isaac and Jacob. Ishmael and Esau were rejected even though they were born of Abraham and Isaac, because they did not believe in Christ.

C. Grace First

The Jews in Paul's day could not understand their failure in the previous dispensation until they understood grace.

D. Israel's Five Curses

Israel's failure resulted in five curses coming on the nation (Leviticus 26:15-46). These are progressive. If the nation still turns from God after each one, another curse comes on them until total dispersion of the nation occurs. Read Leviticus 26:27-39. Jerusalem was dispersed twice in their history: 586-516 BC to Babylon and in 70 AD until 1948 AD after the fall of Jerusalem by Rome. Deuteronomy 28:47-68 is the prophecy which the Jews are under today.

E. Seven Signs of Israel's Coming Judgment

1. The sign of tongues which introduced the Church Age and the stopping of the age of Israel (Isaiah 28:10-13).

2. The virgin birth of Jesus Christ (Isaiah 7:14-16).

3. The betrayal of Messiah (Zechariah 11:12,13).

4. The uniqueness of Messiah's death (Isaiah 53:9). He died twice (spiritually and physically).

5. The resurrection of Messiah (Isaiah 52:13, 53:10).

6. Thirty-eight years of evangelism before the fall of Jerusalem (Malachi 1:5), fulfilled in the book of Acts.

7. The prophecy of the siege of Jerusalem and its fall (Luke 21:20-24, Daniel 9:26).

F. During Israel's Dispersion

The Church Age operates during Israel's dispersion. Israel's curse is on today and God is still protecting the nation. Therefore there is a special curse on any nation who tries to oppress Israel. God's wrath is on them.

II. Explaining Israel to the Gentiles (1–13)

10:1 ⸿ Brethren, my heart's desire and prayer to God for Israel is that they may be saved.

Paul is telling the Roman believers (mainly Gentiles) that he still has a love and concern for his people by birth, Israel. His concern is for their spiritual condition. This should be our prayer also. We are to pray for the peace of Jerusalem (Psalm 122:6) and peace comes through salvation (Romans 5:1).

10:2 For I bear them witness that they have a zeal for God, but not according to knowledge.

For I bear them record (I am a witness) that they have a zeal for God, but not according to knowledge (*epignosis*: revealed knowledge).

This is why Paul prays for their salvation. They are taken over by religion, zeal without knowledge. They have a zeal for anything but the truth of salvation and the truth of the word of God. They have a zeal for tradition (Galatians 1:14), but not for the revelation of the scriptures.

10:3 For they being ignorant of God's righteousness, and seeking to establish their own righteousness, have not submitted to the righteousness of God.

God's righteousness was taught in the Old Testament, during the law. They just did not receive it like the Gentiles did (9:30). Religion always ignores the righteousness of God and goes about to establish man's own righteousness.

Many Christians today are doing the same. They have gone for religion. When you are carnal, you often become religious. The sinner says today, "I will stand on my own righteousness in eternity." All sinners are judged according to their works (Romans 2:6 , Revelation 20:12). Believers will spend eternity in heaven because they have stood on Jesus' works. We cannot be spiritual through our own works. If any part of God's plan depended on man, then God's plan is no better than man's. A chain is only as strong as its weakest link.

10:4 For Christ *is* the end of the law for righteousness to everyone who believes.

Throughout the Old Testament, when a person left the law and believed the word, Christ became the end of the law to them for their salvation. This verse says that faith in Christ is the end of the law, for righteousness. The law has other uses (morality, sanitation, good citizenship) but not anything to produce righteousness.

10:5 ¶ For Moses writes about the righteousness which is of the law, "The man who does those things shall live by them."

For Moses describes the righteousness which is of (from) the law, (see Leviticus 18:5) that the man who does those things shall live by them.

If you choose the law for your savior, you have to live by all the law. If you choose Christ, then you live by Him.

10:6 But the righteousness of faith speaks in this way, "Do not say in your heart, 'Who will ascend into heaven?'" (that is, to bring Christ down *from above*)

But the righteousness of (by) faith speaks in this wise (see Deuteronomy 30:11-14), Say not in your heart, Who shall ascend into heaven? (that is, to bring Christ down from above:)

Righteousness by any other means than faith in Jesus Christ, says "Jesus did not do enough on the cross. I have to help." This means Jesus did not do enough and will have to come back from heaven and finish the work of redemption.

10:7 or, "'Who will descend into the abyss?'" (that is, to bring Christ up from the dead).

Or, Who shall descend into the deep (*sheol*)? (that is, to bring Christ up from the dead.)

If you can be saved by the law, what good is the death, burial, resurrection and ascension of Jesus? The righteousness which is of the law says, "Bring Him down again from heaven, and up from hell." It was all no good, or only partially good. This is blasphemy! So is legalism for salvation or spirituality! Legalism always ignores the work of the cross.

10:8 But what does it say? "The word is near you, in your mouth and in your heart" (that is, the word of faith which we preach):

But what says it? (see Deuteronomy 30:14) The word is near you, in your mouth and in your heart: that is, the word (*rhema*: communicated word) of faith which we preach;

"It" is righteousness which is by faith. Righteousness always speaks! If it is the righteousness of works, then it never acknowledges Jesus' works, but its own. If it is of faith, then it always speaks of the work of Jesus, voice's God's promises. It is believed in the heart and spoken through the mouth.

10:9 that if you confess with your mouth the Lord Jesus and believe in your heart that God has raised Him from the dead, you will be saved.

That if you shall confess (*homologeo*: to say the same thing) with your mouth the Lord Jesus (Jesus as Lord) and shall believe in your heart that God has raised Him from the dead, you shall be saved.

Seeing Jesus as the Son of God always produces salvation. You also acknowledge that God raised Jesus from the dead. The resurrection is the center of God's plan of salvation for mankind (Psalm 16:10, 11, Acts 2:24, Acts 13:30, Romans 8:11, 1 Peter 3:18). This results in salvation (Acts 16:31). Saved is in the future tense. Salvation is the result of a previous action, believing and confessing. The word is also passive voice. You receive salvation. It is a gift of God (Ephesians 2:8, 9).

10:10 For with the heart one believes unto righteousness, and with the mouth confession is made unto salvation.

For with the heart man believes (it is believed) unto (resulting in) righteousness, and with the mouth confession is made unto (resulting in) salvation.

Righteousness is always produced by faith. But the object of faith determines which type of righteousness will be produced. Faith toward the law (human good) produces human righteousness (Isaiah 64:6). Faith toward Jesus Christ always produces righteousness from God.

10:11 For the Scripture says, "Whoever believes on Him will not be put to shame."

For the Scripture says (see Isaiah 28:16), Whosoever believes on Him (Christ) shall not be put to shame.

This refers to the future Great White Throne Judgment. We will never be put to shame after believing on Jesus Christ. This is an Old Testament scripture which shows salvation was the same before the cross as after.

10:12 For there is no distinction between Jew and Greek, for the same Lord over all is rich to all who call upon Him.

For there is no difference between the Jew and Greek (Gentile nations): for the same Lord over all is rich unto all that call upon Him.

Calling on the Lord is the confession of vv. 9 and 10. Jesus is the same Lord to all men, also teaching unlimited atonement.

10:13 For "whoever calls on the name of the Lord shall be saved."

For (continuation of thought) whosoever (Jew or Gentile) shall call on the name of the Lord shall be saved.

III. Church To Do What Israel Did Not (14–21)

Verses 12 and 13 show how Israel failed in the Old Testament to evangelize the world. Verses 14 through 17 show the importance of telling others the gospel.

Before Babel, there was no need for missionary activity, everyone spoke the same language. Abram was the first missionary spoken of in the word. He was called a "Hebrew" (one who crosses the river). He crossed over the Euphrates into Canaan and evangelized. Some of his first converts were Aner, Mamre and Eschol. This began the Israelite race who were responsible for spreading the gospel. They failed as a nation (the theme of Romans 9, 10, and 11) and God turned to all nations during the dispensation of the Gentiles. The Jews by teaching, had to hear. Yet, their hearing of the gospel did not produce faith. They hardened their hearts. Once their heart was hardened, they failed to spread the gospel and spread the law instead.

A. Four Questions
The first three questions are in v. 14.

10:14 ¶ How then shall they call on Him in whom they have not believed? And how shall they believe in Him of whom they have not heard? And how shall they hear without a preacher?

How then shall they call on Him (expression of their faith) in whom they have not believed? and how shall they believe in Him of whom they have not heard? and how shall they hear without a preacher?

1. How shall they call?

2. How shall they believe?

3. How shall they hear (without a preacher)?

Paul traces their salvation back to its beginning or origin. He begins with the final expression of faith and the receiving of salvation, confessing Jesus as Lord with the mouth. The preceding step is believing in Jesus as Lord with the heart, an act of faith which comes from hearing the gospel. The third question brings in the importance of someone, a preacher, someone to give the message.

10: 15 And how shall they preach unless they are sent? As it is written: "How beautiful are the feet of those who preach the gospel of peace, Who bring glad tidings of good things!"

And how shall they preach except they are sent? as it is written, (Isaiah

52:7) How beautiful are the feet of them that preach the gospel of peace, and bring glad tidings of good things!

4. How can they preach?
The gospel is not the proclaiming of law or human rules, but the introduction of good things, peace.

B. The Gospel and the Law

10:16 But they have not all obeyed the gospel. For Isaiah says, "Lord, who has believed our report?"

But they have not all obeyed the gospel. For Isaiah says (in 53:1), Lord, who has believed our report?

Israel, who was supposed to be the preacher, was not even a believer. They did not hear their own message and believe it. Only a remnant believed and saved the nation. Isaiah was a proclaimer of the gospel and wondered who was believing. The end of this chapter indicates the Jews did not believe as a whole, but the Gentiles did.

10:17 So then faith *comes* by hearing, and hearing by the word of God.

So then (conclusion of the questions) faith comes by hearing (the report), and hearing by the word (*rhema*: communicated word) of God.

It is not the message, but the content of the message which contains the power. If the content of the gospel is the word of God, it is then backed by the power of God (Romans 1:16).

10:18 ¶ But I say, have they not heard? Yes indeed: "Their sound has gone out to all the earth, And their words to the ends of the world."

The world was evangelized despite Israel's failure to preach the gospel. God is not stopped because we will not go. He is not dependent on us, but we are on Him. The voice of those who would go, a remnant of Jews and a number of saved Gentiles, went into all the earth (inhabited world). The few who did go were spoken of by God as a blessing.

10:19 ¶ But I say, did Israel not know? First Moses says: "I will

provoke you to jealousy by *those who are* not a nation, I will move you to anger by a foolish nation."

But I say, Did Israel not know? First Moses says (in Deuteronomy 32:21): I will provoke you to jealousy by them that are no people, and by a foolish nation I will anger you.

Yes, Israel knew. God told them in the Old Testament they were rebellious. He also told them the Gentiles would be evangelized even if Israel refused to tell (Deuteronomy 32:21, Isaiah 65:1,2). Most of the Jews considered Gentiles to be of no value and ignorant.

10:20 ¶But Isaiah is very bold and says: "I was found by those who did not seek Me; I was made manifest to those who did not ask for Me."

But Isaiah is very bold and says (in 65:1), I was found of them that sought Me not (Gentiles); I was made manifest unto them that did asked not for Me.

The Gentiles did not actively seek after God as did the Jews, but they did seek God aside from the law. The Jews who did actively seek God, sought Him through the law and missed the righteousness God intended them to have (Romans 9:30-32).

10:21 ¶ But to Israel he says: "All day long I have stretched out My hands to a disobedient and contrary people."

But to Israel he says (in 65:2): All day long I have stretched forth My hands unto a disobedient and gainsaying (contrary or back talking) people.

God did not have to do much to manifest Himself to Gentiles. But He went out of His way for a long period of time with the stubborn Jews to show Himself and His plan.

11:1–36 Israel: Past, Present, and Future

This is the final chapter of three parenthetical chapters (Romans 9-11) showing God's purpose for Israel in the past, their present position in the world and His plan for them in the future.

I. Past (1–6)

God's dealing with the remnant of Jews who believe in Jesus Christ has never changed from Old Testament to New. They are part of the reason Israel still exists and will continue to exist as part of God's eternal plan for the nation of Israel. Even in the worst of times for the nation, there has been a group of Jews who believe in the Lord for their salvation, even if that group was only a few. When the Church began, God only allowed Israel to be dispersed, not destroyed. He has put the nation on a shelf until the times of the Gentiles are fulfilled. Israel will again become the center of God's plan for world evangelism and discipleship when the Church has been taken from the world at the Rapture. He will not allow Israel to be destroyed during the tribulation or at the Battle of Armageddon, again because of the remnant of believing Jews who accept Jesus as their Savior, during the tribulation.

A. God Does Not Cast Away

11:1 ¶ I say then, has God cast away His people? Certainly not! For I also am an Israelite, of the seed of Abraham, of the tribe of Benjamin.

I say then (conclusion after chapter 10), Has God cast away his people? God forbid (emphatically not). For I also am an Israelite, of the seed of Abraham (physical Jew), of the tribe of Benjamin (Philippians 3:5-6).

God can never cast them away. God cannot change. The Jewish race has a future no matter how much they have rejected God. God never forgets, or leaves His own. Israel became a type, a symbol, of God's grace to believers. He foreknew Israel (v. 2) and He foreknew us (Ephesians 1:4). God also has a plan for Israel as much as He has a plan for Church Age believers today.

11:2 God has not cast away His people whom He foreknew. Or do you not know what the Scripture says of Elijah, how he pleads with God against Israel, saying,

Salvation from its very inception (before the foundation of the world) is the plan of God. Man had no part because it would then be subject to failure. Man can only receive a past completed perfect work. Once you enter into His plan, you are kept by His power which is omnipotent (1 Peter 1:4-5).

God's keeping power is going to be illustrated from one of the greatest times of apostasy in the northern kingdom under Ahab. The apostasy was so bad that Elijah interceded against for God to destroy Israel for the way the nation was treating Him.

11:3 "Lord, they have killed Your prophets and torn down Your altars, and I alone am left, and they seek my life"?

Lord, they (Israel) have killed your prophets, and torn down your altars; and I am left alone, and they seek my life (see 1 Kings 19:10-18).

Elijah was not only jealous for the nation of Israel, he was also feeling sorry for himself as he sat in a cave refusing to go back to the place of his calling. Twice, God tried to get Elijah to return home, but he continued with the story of pity toward himself and blame toward Israel. He told the Lord he was the only person left serving God. All the rest of the nation had turned to serving Baal and idols.

11:4 But what does the divine response say to him? "I have reserved for Myself seven thousand men who have not bowed the knee to Baal."

But what was God's answer to him? I have reserved to myself (unknown to anyone) seven thousand men, who have not bowed their knee to the image of Baal.

During the times of greatest apostasy there is always a remnant according to the election of grace (Isaiah 1:9). As it was in the times of Elijah, it is today and will be until the Second Advent of the Lord. God has always foreknown that Israel would have a believing remnant. Even after the Rapture of the Church, the remnant will reappear; 144,000 Jews will accept the Lord and begin evangelizing in Israel and among the Gentile nations.

B. The Remnant

11:5 Even so then, at this present time there is a remnant

according to the election of grace.

Even so then at this present time (Church Age) also there is a remnant according to the election of grace.

This is why the Church cannot go under or be destroyed today. There are always prophets of destruction saying God is through with the Church, but this is impossible. Jesus said, the gates of hell would not prevail against the Church (Matthew 16:18). So how could governments, religion or even unbelief in the Church cause it to be destroyed? Through the Dark Ages, the Church survived because there were a few who had accepted Jesus as their Savior and were trusting God for the truth to be revealed even in the midst of religious darkness.

11:6 And if by grace, then *it is* no longer of works; otherwise grace is no longer grace. But if *it is* of works, it is no longer grace; otherwise work is no longer work.

And if it is by grace (the elect, the remnant), then is it no more of works: otherwise grace is no more grace. But if it is of works, then is it no more grace: otherwise work is no more work.

A little leaven destroys the lump. You cannot mix your works into the plan of God's grace. The remnant of Israel did not make themselves the remnant, God did through their faith. But God foreknew, and elected them before they believed. God's plan is not subject to Israel. God's plan is not subject to us, the Church. God's plan is subject to Himself. We are allowed to enter into His perfect plan. It is grace or works, never grace and works.

II. Present (7–25)

11:7 ¶ What then? Israel has not obtained what it seeks; but the elect have obtained it, and the rest were blinded.

What then? Israel has not obtained that which he seeks for; but the election has obtained it, and the rest were blinded (hardened—see 9:18, 11:25, 2 Corinthians 4:4).

Not all Israel (nationally) is Israel (true believers). Ephesians 2:12 says that Gentiles who were not born again were strangers from the commonwealth of Israel. These are believers in the Jewish nation.

The hardness of Israel today is like Pharaoh of Egyptian times. Through his hardness the gospel was spread fast (not because of his hardness). A showdown always causes a crowd to come. Israel today as a whole is hardened against Jesus and a showdown is coming. At Armageddon, God will win in front of a large crowd as He did with Pharaoh before the Jews and the Egyptian people.

A. Points on Election

1. Christians were elected in eternity past by God the Father (Isaiah 42:1, Peter 2:6).

2. This election took place before man existed (Ephesians 1:4, 2 Thessalonians 2:13, 1 Peter 1:2).

3. It is the present and future possession of every believer (Colossians 3:12).

4. Every believer shares the election of Christ (Romans 8:28-33).

5. Election for us takes place at the moment of salvation (2 Thessalonians 2:13, 1 Corinthians 1:9).

6. Election is the foundation of the Church (1 Thessalonians 1:4).

7. Election has a purpose, that Jesus might have representation in the earth during His absence (Galatians 5:8).

11:8 Just as it is written: "God has given them a spirit of stupor, eyes that they should not see and ears that they should not hear, to this very day."

(According as it is written, God has given them the spirit of slumber, eyes that they should not see, and ears that they should not hear;) until this day (see Isaiah 29:10).

Throughout the Church Age, the Jewish nation as a whole have the faculty for understanding, but it will not function properly. This has come because of blindness from Satan they allowed by their rejection of the gospel.

11:9 ¶ And David says: "Let their table become a snare and a trap, a stumbling block and a recompense to them.

And David says (in Psalm 69:22-23), Let their table (Passover table, rights and rituals of Christ) be made a snare, and a trap, and a stumbling block, and a recompense (retribution, payback) to them:

Each time devout Jewish people have their feasts, fasts and rituals, they have a picture of the person and work of Jesus in front of them, but they cannot see its meaning. They have been blinded by their rejection of Jesus.

11:10 Let their eyes be darkened, so that they do not see, and bow down their back always."

Let their eyes (understanding) be darkened, that they may not see (perceive), and bow down their back (be slaves) always.

The eyes are a reference to the mind, the perception (Matthew 5:29, 6:22, 7:3-5, 2 Corinthians 4:4, Ephesians 1:18, James 1:8).

B. Israel's Failure the Gentile's Riches

Verse 11 now asks, "Does Israel have a future? Have they stumbled forever?"

11:11 ¶ I say then, have they stumbled that they should fall? Certainly not! But through their fall, to provoke them to jealousy, salvation *has come* to the Gentiles.

I say then, Have they stumbled that they should fall? God forbid (emphatically not): but rather through their fall (trespass) salvation is come to the Gentiles, for to provoke them to jealousy.

Israel has a future. Their rejection was fully seen when the Jewish religious crowd crucified Jesus. God through their rejection, turned to the Gentiles. Cursing became a blessing. The Jews were dispersed and will be through the Church Age. Once the Church is gone (Rapture), God will again turn to the Jews for seven more years (Tribulation). The Jewish nation will again be the custodians of the gospel and the word of God. A remnant will reappear (144,000 Jewish believers) and many Jews and Gentiles will be born again. At the Second Advent, the born again Jews and Gentiles will be used to populate the earth during the millennium.

11:12 Now if their fall *is* riches for the world, and their failure riches for the Gentiles, how much more their fullness!

Now if the fall (trespass) of them is the riches of the world (*kosmos*: worlds system), and the diminishing (default) of them the riches of the Gentiles;

how much more their fullness (the Second Advent)?

When Israel was dispersed, the Church was formed and became world-wide. Also the Jews were tight fisted with the gospel, and the Church was God's new means to release the word.

God always turns cursing into blessing (Romans 8:28) for His people. There is a profit to the world by the fall of the Jews naturally and spiritually. Their fall (natural) and diminishing (spiritual default) is riches of the rest of the world. God has turned to the Gentile nations to spread the gospel and take the word for discipleship to them also. Great spiritual and natural bless-ings have come to the world as God turned from Israel to the Gentiles on the Day of Pentecost.

But for the Jewish nation, they still exist whether they have a homeland or not. Today, they do. The Jewish people have been scattered among the na-tions since the time of the destruction of Jerusalem and the temple in 70 AD. Nations and races have come and gone, but God's truth about Israel has never changed. They cannot be destroyed. They are a race today and have a future according to God's word.

11:13 ¶ For I speak to you Gentiles; inasmuch as I am an apostle to the Gentiles, I magnify my ministry,

For I speak to you Gentiles, inasmuch as I am the apostle of the Gentiles, I magnify my office (apostle):

Paul will magnify his calling, not his personality. His calling comes from God, his personality from natural birth.

11:14 if by any means I may provoke to jealousy *those who are* my flesh and save some of them.

If by any means I may provoke to emulation (jealousy see v. 11) those who are my flesh (natural Jews), and might save some of them.

The more Gentiles that are born again and are blessed through the min-istry of the Church today, the more potential there is for Jews to become jealous (in a good sense) and be blessed also. Jealousy could be the best thing to happen to a Jew searching for God, and through the jealousy find Jesus as his Messiah and Lord. The best thing Paul can do for the Jew is to be an apostle to the Gentiles. More Jews have been saved since the Church began than during the age of Israel.

11:15 For if their being cast away *is* the reconciling of the world, what *will* their acceptance *be* but life from the dead?

For if the casting away of them be the reconciling of the (rest of the) world, what shall the receiving of them be, but life from the dead (the new birth)?

If God turned from the Jewish nation and toward the rest of the world, how glorious will the day be when God again turns to Israel and they find their Messiah to be the One they rejected? It will be the beginning of the Millennium.

11:16 ¶ For if the firstfruit *is* holy, the lump *is* also *holy*; and if the root *is* holy, so *are* the branches.

The founding of the Jewish nation was Abraham accepting the Lord by faith. His son Isaac and grandson Jacob also accepted the Lord by faith as did all twelve sons of Jacob, the tribes of Israel. This is the firstfruits, the Fathers of Israel.

Then throughout Old Testament history, there has always been a remnant of Jews who found the Lord as their Savior. This is the lump, the part of Israel who also found true salvation despite the presence of the law. This is the part of the nation of Israel who are true Israel.

The root, from which sprang Abraham as well as the Church, is the Lord Jesus. The branches which came from Him are Jewish and Gentile alike, anyone who accepts Him and finds eternal life. The common denominator is not Abraham or Moses, but the Lord Jesus and faith in Him.

11:17 And if some of the branches were broken off, and you, being a wild olive tree, were grafted in among them, and with them became a partaker of the root and fatness of the olive tree,

Wild olive branches come from wild olive trees. Until the time of Abraham, there were no Jews, just Gentiles. All mankind came from a wild olive tree whose root was Adam. Abraham was a Gentile until the time he became a Jew through faith in Jesus Christ (Jehovah). At that point, he was broken from the wild olive tree and grafted to the root of a new tree, the Lord Jesus Christ. Through Isaac and Jacob, a new trunk was formed. Branches began to grow from the tree all of whom received the Lord Jesus. Anyone who did not receive the Lord (Jew or Gentile) were part of the wild olive tree. Anyone who did receive the Lord were part of the new tree. Gentiles who were saved in the Old Testament became part of the true Israel. Joseph married a believing Egyptian and gave birth to two half tribes of Israel, Ephraim and Manasseh. Moses married a believing Ethiopian. A large mixed multitude of believing Egyptians joined Israel as they left Egypt and headed toward Canaan. Rahab and Ruth became part of the lineage of David and eventually Jesus Himself. They were later joined by Bathsheba (Matthew 1). The list goes on proving that God is not, and never has been, a respecter of persons. He is a respecter of faith. Anyone (Jew or Gentile) can accept Jesus as their Savior and become a partaker of the fatness, blessings and prosperity, of the family of God.

In eternity, your physical birth, position in society, education, wealth or works will not get you into heaven. You will not be judged for heaven based on you as an individual. You are allowed into heaven or sent to the lake of fire based on which tree you are part of. You were born into a dead tree and needed to be born again (grafted into) a living tree. If you did that, you are no longer a part of the dead tree of Adam, but the living tree of Jesus Christ. In Adam all die. In Christ all will be made alive.

11:18 do not boast against the branches. But if you do boast, *remember that* you do not support the root, but the root *supports you.*

Do not boast (speak out) against the branches (the new tree). But if you boast, you do not bear the root (Jesus), but the root (bears) you.

This is a warning for the believer not to pick up the attitude of the unbeliever, the world. Two major opinions toward God are magnified in the world —hatred toward the Jewish nation and hatred toward the Church of Jesus Christ. Sadly, many Christians join in with antisemitism and speaking evil of dedicated believers. Paul warns believers here that they are not helping the cause of Jesus Christ, but hindering it. Jesus does not need our help, we need His. The only way we can help the cause of Jesus is to spread the gospel to Jews and Gentiles and give great respect to the nation of Israel for the future they have yet to experience. This is how God sees Israel and the Church and how we too should see them too.

11:19 ¶ You will say then, "Branches were broken off that I might be grafted in."

You (arrogant believer) will say then, The branches were broken off, that I might be grafted in.

This is a stupid believer, thinking God is a respecter of persons, namely him. i.e. "God turned away from the Jewish nation, just for me."

11:20 Well *said*. Because of unbelief they were broken off, and you stand by faith. Do not be haughty, but fear.

God is not a respecter of persons, but a respecter of faith. Not only were you born again by faith, but you are to walk each day by faith. Faith comes by hearing and hearing by the word of God (10:17). This is simply a command to continue daily in God's word. If you do, you will think straight and not come up with such stupid comments like, "God loves me more than the Jews."

11:21 For if God did not spare the natural branches, He may not spare you either.

For if God spared not the natural branches (Jewish unbelievers), take heed lest he also will not spare you (Gentile unbelievers).

If you are an unbeliever and a Gentile, do not play the same game the Jews did in the Old Testament. Do not think God turned from the Jewish nation because you are better or more highly favored. You will not get into heaven in the Church Age because you are a Gentile anymore than the Jews of the Old Covenant could get into heaven because they were Jews. Jews as well as Gentiles are favored by God because of faith. They will be equally judged to an eternity apart from God because of their unbelief, rejection of Jesus as their Savior.

11:22 Therefore consider the goodness and severity of God: on those who fell, severity; but toward you, goodness, if you continue in *His* goodness. Otherwise you also will be cut off.

Behold (consider) therefore the goodness and severity of God: on them which fell, severity; but toward you, goodness, if you continue in his goodness: otherwise you also will be cut off (out).

God's goodness today is turned mainly toward the Gentile nations who make up the church along with a remnant of believing Jews. This is the Church God is using today. Israel fell, turning as a whole against the Lord, and God in His severity turned from them to minister to the world through the Gentile nations. This is God's severity toward Israel and goodness toward the Church. Israel faced God's severity because they did not continue in God's goodness, His grace. They became apathetic and rested in their works instead of God's works.

The Church, or each individual member of it, could face the same consequence. If we do not continue in God's goodness, we could face His severity also and be removed from usefulness as a member of the Body of Christ. This verse is not teaching that a disobedient member of the Body of Christ is removed from the Church, or cut off to become a sinner again. The Greek word means to be cut out. As Israel was cut out of God's plan for ministry, so could the Church. Any Christian who becomes carnal and remains so, will face God's displeasure and could face His discipline. One thing which is for sure, the carnal Christian is no longer controlled by the Holy Spirit and is not useful for God's plan of ministry.

> **11:23 And they also, if they do not continue in unbelief, will be grafted in, for God is able to graft them in again.**

And they (Israel) also, if they abide not still in unbelief (receive the Lord as Savior), shall be grafted in: for God is able to graft them in again.

Any Jew today who believes in Jesus Christ for salvation, is made a part of the Church, the Body of Christ. They are grafted into the tree being used to do God's will in the earth of evangelizing and discipling believers.

> **11:24 For if you were cut out of the olive tree which is wild by nature, and were grafted contrary to nature into a cultivated olive tree, how much more will these, who *are* natural *branches*, be grafted into their own olive tree?**

For if you (believing Jews) were cut out of the olive tree which is wild by nature, and were grafted contrary to nature into a good olive tree (the Church): how much more shall these, which be (are) the natural branches (physical Jews), be grafted into their own olive tree?

This verse is setting up the next verse, telling that the Church is only a temporary part of God's plan for evangelism in the earth. When the time for the Church has come to an end, Christians will be raptured and Israel will again take its place and finish its job as custodians of the gospel and the teaching of the word of God. The good olive tree will be removed and the wild tree will again pick up the mantle of preaching the gospel to the world.

11:25 ¶ For I do not desire, brethren, that you should be ignorant of this mystery, lest you should be wise in your own opinion, that blindness in part has happened to Israel until the fullness of the Gentiles has come in.

For I do not desire, brethren, that you should be ignorant of this mystery, lest you should be wise in your own conceits (opinions); that blindness (*porousis*: callousness) in part is happened (*ginomai*: come to pass) to Israel, until the fullness of the Gentiles be come in.

When the word "mystery" appears in the New Testament, it is not referring to something we do not know. It is speaking about something unknown in the Old Testament now revealed in the New. Since the Church Age was unknown in the Old Testament, a mystery, it is obvious that the blindness of Israel during the time must be a mystery also. The fullness of the Gentiles will end at the Rapture of the Church, the partial blindness on Israel will be lifted and the revelation of Jesus as Messiah will be known to the Jewish nation. This blindness has caused Israel to become hardened, callous toward the truth of the gospel. This blindness is from Satan of course (2 Corinthians 4:4), but God has not lifted it because of Israel's rejection of Jesus at His first coming. It will be lifted soon at the coming of Jesus for the Church.

III. Future (25–36)

A. All Israel
The remnant according to election of grace will occupy the earth during the millennium. They are called "all Israel."

11:26 And so all Israel will be saved, as it is written: "The Deliverer will come out of Zion, and He will turn away ungodliness from Jacob;

And so all Israel shall be saved (spared, delivered): as it is written (Isaiah 59:20), There shall come out of Zion the Deliverer (Second Advent), and shall turn away ungodliness from Jacob (remove all sinners):

"All Israel" is a title for the remnant, the believing portion of the Jewish nation. "Jacob" was his name before he was saved. After his wrestling match with the Lord Jesus and his loss to Him, his name was changed to "Israel." Throughout the Old Testament, the believing remnant and the unbelieving majority are referred to as, "O house of Jacob(unbelievers), O house of Israel (believers)." Jews who have been saved throughout history will receive a resurrection body at the end of the Tribulation. Those who are saved during the Tribulation and endure to the end (the Second Advent of Jesus) will go into the millennium and help repopulate the earth with natural people. These groups of Jews make up the group called "all Israel."

11:27 For this is My covenant with them, when I take away their sins."

For this is my covenant to them (saved Jews from all dispensations), when I shall take away their sins.

All covenants to Israel will be fulfilled at the Second Advent of Jesus. Israel will reap their benefits throughout the millennium.

11:28 ¶ Concerning the gospel *they are* enemies for your sake, but concerning the election *they are* beloved for the sake of the fathers.

As concerning the gospel, they are enemies for your sakes (because of you): but as touching the election (born-again Jews), they are beloved for the fathers' (Abraham, Isaac, Jacob) sakes.

Today, Judaism is the enemy of the gospel. It is no more Christianity than any religion of the world. Judaism, like all other religions, teaches salvation by works and thus is in opposition to the gospel. Judaism was the opposer to Jesus, Paul, Peter and the other ministers of the New Testament. Born-again Jews are not part of Judaism, but of the Church. They are not our enemies but fellow believers and fellow soldiers in the work of God. We are as much tied to the Jewish fathers as they are (Galatians 3:29).

11:29 For the gifts and the calling of God *are* irrevocable.

For the gifts (covenants) and calling (salvation) of God are without repentance.

God has no regrets for either the covenants or plan of salvation He offered to the Jewish people and the Gentiles today. If God has no regrets over the Jews, He certainly has no regrets for our gifts and callings. With a perfect plan there can be no regrets.

B. The Perfect Plan of God

Verses 30 through 32 teach of the plan of God. It always glorifies God (v. 36).

11:30 For as you were once disobedient to God, yet have now obtained mercy through their disobedience,

For as you in times past (pre-salvation) have not believed God, yet have now obtained mercy through their unbelief:

Through the unbelief of Israel, God has now turned His full attention toward the Gentiles and the building of the Church.

11:31 even so these also have now been disobedient, that through the mercy shown you they also may obtain mercy.

Even so have these also (unbelieving Jews) now not believed, that through your mercy they also may obtain mercy.

During the Old Testament, the Jews were custodians of the word and were missionaries to the Gentiles. Today, the Gentiles are the custodians and missionaries to the Jews.

11:32 For God has committed them all to disobedience, that He might have mercy on all.

For God has concluded them all (jailed them all, Jews and Gentiles) in unbelief, that he might have mercy on all.

There can be no universal salvation without universal condemnation. All men are under sin, so that redemption can be offered to all. Man is faced with a decision between two eternal destinies, heaven or the lake of fire. All who are in prison is the result of Adam's transgression (Romans 5:12). We are in prison from natural birth. Jesus opened the door for all. He had mercy on all. With all the differences between the Jew and Gentile, Paul wants to clear up that an unbelieving Jew has the same eternal destiny as an unbelieving Gentile, the lake of fire. A believing Jew has the same eternal destiny as a believing Gentile, heaven.
In verses 33 through 36, Paul offers a tremendous praise to God for His perfect plan.

11:33 ¶ Oh, the depth of the riches both of the wisdom and knowledge of God! How unsearchable *are* His judgments and His ways past finding out!

O the depth of the riches both of the wisdom and knowledge of God! how unsearchable are his judgments, and his ways (paths) past finding out (untrackable)!

God's knowledge existed from eternity past He knew all problems and answers we would ever face and need. His wisdom was shown in the fall Adam and the work of Jesus to answer the problem. His wisdom and knowledge are bottomless. His ways are like an animal which cannot be tracked. It is useless to try to figure out how God works.
Jesus said in John 3, the Holy Spirit was like the wind which we cannot see where it comes from or where it goes. Take God at His word and let Him be God. You cannot become saved or spiritual by following on someone else's heels. You must go to the word for yourself.

11:34 "For who has known the mind of the Lord? Or who has become His counselor?"

For who has known the mind of the Lord? or who has been his counselor? (see Isaiah 40: 13, 14)

You cannot second guess God. You must simply accept His perfect plan. God is the ultimate source of help and counsel. No one has ever had to counsel God, or could. If they did, that would mean God needs help. How could a perfect God need help?

11:35 "Or who has first given to Him and it shall be repaid to him?"

Or who has first given to him, and it shall be recompensed (paid back) to him again?

God owes no one. If we gave God help, He would owe us. God is the source of all things. Even what you have to give God—your strength, time, finances —came from Him in the first place. This is grace.

11:36 ¶ For of Him and through Him and to Him *are* all things, to whom *be* glory forever. Amen.

For of (from)him, and through him, and to him, are all things: to whom be glory for ever. Amen.

We have a cycle. All things originate from God the Father. They then come to us through Jesus Christ which gives us the provisions to give back to God.

The Father is the beginning and ending of all things. A perfect plan always glorifies the maker. God's plan always glorifies God.

Even our faith, with which we receive provisions from God, gives Him glory (see Romans 4:20).

12:1–21 Members of God's Body

I. Living Sacrifice (1–12)

This chapter starts with the true use of our body. We have seen the faults of the flesh, now we have the power of the body as an instrument for the Lord.

There is no such thing as a one shot dedication, surrendering to preach, rededication or presenting yourself for full-time Christian service. Dedication is a process which goes on throughout your entire life. There are always weaknesses which can only be dealt with and corrected by the word, then your choice to act on it.

There is no such thing as one meal which will last for a lifetime. We must eat every day. Decisions are made each day of what to eat, when to eat, whether to eat at all, etc. The Christian life is never one decision and that is all. You make decisions every day to study the word, what to study, when to study, etc. This way your body is a living (perpetual) sacrifice to God.

> **12:1 ¶ I beseech you therefore, brethren, by the mercies of God, that you present your bodies a living sacrifice, holy, acceptable to God, *which is* your reasonable service.**

I beseech you therefore, brethren, by the mercies of God, that you present your bodies a living sacrifice, holy (separated unto God), acceptable (well pleasing) unto God, which is your reasonable (*logikos*: logical, rational) service.

Paul asks us to present our bodies. The Greek word means to yield (see 6:13, 16, 19). Yielding is not an emotional function, but a giving up, presenting of something. Here it is our bodies as a servant for the indwelling Holy Spirit and the renewed mind.

This verse is a conclusion and appeal by Paul to do the only logical thing after Chapters 6 through 11. After defining the problem with the sin nature, the flesh, and how to have victory over it, there is only one conclusion. Use your body for God, directed by His Spirit and His word. Chapter 12 is the introduction to the remainder of the book. It is a result of dedication, a yielded body for service to God.

This verse is not a one shot emotional dedication used by a group of Christians standing around a campfire making a vow to God to serve Him for the rest of their lives. This verse is only the beginning of a lifelong change, not the conclusion. Verse 1 cannot stand on its own, but must be used in connection with verse 2. Verse 1 tells you what to do, but not how to do it. Verse 2 is the instructions telling you how to present your body as a living sacrifice.

A living sacrifice is a paradox. You cannot have a sacrifice which is alive. But if you see the inner man as alive, and the outer man as dead unto the world and sin, this verse suddenly makes sense.

A. Present Your Bodies
The first half of the verse is what not to do. The second half is what to do.

12:2 And do not be conformed to this world, but be transformed by the renewing of your mind, that you may prove what *is* that good and acceptable and perfect will of God.

And be not conformed (molded) to this world: but be transformed (*metamorphoo*: metamorphosis, changed) by the renewing of your mind, that ye may prove what is that good, and acceptable, and perfect, will of God.

Don't be molded from outward pressure of the world, but be transformed from the inside. The key to maturity is to stop being alarmed or even impressed with circumstances. Instead, be changed by what the word of God has to say about life. Circumstances can change and often do. But, the word of God never changes and cannot. Circumstances will never change the word of God, but the word of God will change circumstances.

The renewing of the mind, learning to think according to scripture, having the mind of Christ, is one of the real keys to success in the Christian life. This maturity helps you see life as it truly is and move through circumstances as Jesus Himself did when He was on earth.

A renewed mind also helps you mature in the ever improving will of God for your life. You begin in the good will of God, progress into the more acceptable will of God and finally end up in the perfect will of God. Paul began his spiritual walk with God by studying the word of God. He then became a teacher and apostle, working in churches in the areas around Jerusalem and Israel. He began to establish churches and eventually found his "high calling," writing over half of the New Testament and impacting lives forever. This came about through a renewed mind, sensitive to the voice of the Holy Spirit.

12:3 ¶ For I say, through the grace given to me, to everyone who is among you, not to think *of himself* more highly than he

ought to think, but to think soberly, as God has dealt to each one a measure of faith.

For I say, through the grace (*charis*: Paul's office of apostle) given to me, to every man that is among you, not to think of himself more highly than he ought to think; but to think soberly (in a stabilized manner), according as God hath dealt to every man the measure of faith.

Paul's grace was the five-fold office of the apostle. Paul was speaking to the Ephesian believers, from his office to theirs (v. 4). This word carries much spiritual weight. Before Paul tells them about their office titles, he tells them of the attitude which must back their position in the body of Christ: humility.

Paul did not say it was wrong to think highly of yourself, just not to think more highly than your ought to think. Spiritual self-esteem is acceptable to God, respecting what God has done in your life. Thinking too highly of yourself begins to think you are responsible for your call, your wisdom and anointing. All of these come from God and all glory for anything in your life belongs to Him. The enemy of maturity is arrogance. Paul is simply saying, "think grace thoughts."

Verse 3 is explaining our similarities, the common measure of faith.

B. Different Spiritual Offices
Verses 4 through 8 explains our differences, spiritual offices in the body of Christ.

12:4 For as we have many members in one body, but all the members do not have the same function,

As much as Paul had an office, so does every member of the body of Christ. Paul is speaking from his office as apostle to our individual offices. He called his office a grace (v. 3) and so are our offices (v. 6). Since our offices are a part of God's grace, they come from God the Father, the author of grace (1 Corinthians 12:28) and are overseen by the Lord Jesus Christ (1 Corinthians 12:5, Ephesians 4:1).

12:5 so we, *being* many, are one body in Christ, and individually members of one another.

The Body of Christ is a team, made up of individual ministers working together. We do not all play the same position, but each form an integral part to accomplish the will of God in the earth.

C. Gifts and Offices

1. Spiritual gifts and offices are taught in 1 Corinthians 12, Ephesians 4 and Romans 12.

2. They are the Father's witness to the plan of salvation (Hebrews 2:4).

3. The purpose of the ministry offices and spiritual gifts is declared in Ephesians 4:8-13, the perfecting and equipping of the saints.

4. The perspective of spiritual gifts and offices are found in 1 Corinthians 12:1-13

5. The gifts are permanent as long as the Church is in the earth. They were given at the resurrection of Jesus and will removed at His return.

6. God's attitude toward these gifts is found in Romans 12.

7. The fuel for the gifts to operate is love from the believer who is in fellowship or spiritual.

12:6 Having then gifts differing according to the grace that is given to us, *let us use them*: if prophecy, *let us prophesy* in proportion to our faith;

Having then gifts differing according to the grace (our spiritual office) that is given to us, whether prophecy, let us prophesy according to the proportion of faith;

This verse teaches something simple which is often overlooked. We believe the gifts of the Spirit are something we can hand select because 1 Corinthians 12:31 tells us to "covet earnestly the best gifts." The best gifts are not the ones we choose, but the ones which accompany our office and bring it to maximum production. The gifts we operate in are determined by the office we stand in. "Having gifts (of the Spirit) differing according to the grace (office) that is given to us." Once it is revealed to us what office we stand in, then we are to desire the best gifts to enhance that office.

The first ministry office mentioned is prophecy. This is not the office of the prophet (Ephesians 4:11), but one who operates in the simple gift of prophecy (1 Corinthians 12:10, 14:4). The office of the prophet is available to those with a full-time ministry calling. The one who prophesies can be any member of the congregation used during a service, or with any person outside the service. He gives an inspired utterance of exhortation, edification, or comfort (1 Corinthians 14:3,4). General prophecy, which this ministry is, is forthtelling, or the giving forth of a message of edification.

The office of a full time prophet is foretelling, or telling of coming trouble or blessing. This verse again is general prophecy for uplifting of individuals, groups or the congregation of saints.

Because you operate in the simple gift of prophecy does not make you a prophet. Yet, on the other hand, no prophet ever began without prophesying. The offices listed in these verses are for any member of the spirit filled Christian community. They are a launching pad or a stepping stone into the full time ministry if the call is there.

12:7 or ministry, *let us use it* in *our* ministering; he who teaches, in teaching;

Or ministry (*diakonos*: deacon, server), let us wait on our ministering: or he who teaches, on teaching;

Ministry is the spiritual office of a deacon (Acts 6:1-7, 1 Timothy 3:8-16). This is a ministry of service, or helps (1 Corinthians 12:28). This would include ushering, greeting, stacking chairs or working to care for the needs of others in the church service or any church function.

Teaching is the simple gift of teaching, not necessarily the full time ministry office of a teacher (1 Corinthians 12:29, Ephesians 4:11). These are those inclined, or apt to teach (1 Timothy 3:2) who feel most comfortable teaching groups of Christians in home groups, individual classes in church or other Christian functions. They may never reach the full-time office of a teacher, but again, no full-time teacher ever began without teaching a class or home group.

12:8 he who exhorts, in exhortation; he who gives, with liberality; he who leads, with diligence; he who shows mercy, with cheerfulness.

Or he who exhorts, on exhortation: he who gives, let him do it with simplicity (not for outward show); he who rules, with diligence (eagerness); he who shows mercy, with cheerfulness.

An exhorter is one who can easily encourage others and evangelize. Although we are all supposed to evangelize, fulfill the great commission, some are more gifted at soul winning than others. Even pastors are commanded to "do the work of an evangelist" (2 Timothy 4:5) even though they are not evangelists. This would easily be the stair step ministry into the office of the evangelist, if the full time calling was present. Not every person gifted at soul winning is an evangelist, but no evangelist ever began without winning souls.

The next office, given to the body of Christ is the giver. This is the person gifted at making money to place large amounts into church work, evangelism and taking care of those in need. We are all supposed to give tithes and offerings. So this office does not remove our responsibility to give. Yet, there will always be those who can raise and give large amounts of money to help fulfill the great commission and take care of those in need who cannot help themselves. As Jesus told us, when we give, we should do it "not to be seen of men" (Matthew 6:1). This is the admonition to the giver, "not for outward show."

A ruler is next, the office of elders and bishops. These are offices which stand beside the pastor and help with the spiritual oversight in a church. This would be associate pastors, superintendents, and governments (1 Corinthians 12:28).

The final office mentioned is one of compassion, those gifted with mercy. We are all supposed to be merciful (Luke 6:36), but some are specially gifted at taking the hurts and cares off others and replacing it with joy. Jesus made special comment about this person when He mentioned those who came to see Him in prison, and when He was sick, hungry and thirsty (Matthew 25:35,36). This person must strive not to pick up the attitude of the one they are helping. They must keep an attitude of cheerfulness.

12:9 ¶ *Let* love *be* without hypocrisy. Abhor what is evil. Cling to what is good.

Let love be without dissimulation (hypocrisy). Abhor (hate) that which is evil; cleave (cling) to that which is good.

Love should not be an outward show to mask our inward desire to be seen of people and appreciated. This is playing the part of a hypocrite (Galatians 2:13, 2 Corinthians 6:6, 1 Timothy 1:5). Right and wrong actions are always placed before us. We are to hate the evil we see each day, then find the good and cling to it.

12:10 *Be* kindly affectionate to one another with brotherly love, in honor giving preference to one another;

Be kindly affectioned (have a family affection) one to another with brotherly love (*philos*); in honor (respect) preferring (deferring to) one another;

Don't prefer one another for your own gain. Think of others and honor them as a servant to the master. Don't flatter others, but give them true praise.

12:11 not lagging in diligence, fervent in spirit, serving the Lord;

Not slothful in business (slow in zeal); fervent in spirit (at the boiling point in attitude); serving the Lord;

Don't be zealous just for emotional reasons, but to serve the Lord. Be zealous for a good reason!

12:12 rejoicing in hope, patient in tribulation, continuing steadfastly in prayer;

Rejoicing in hope; patient in tribulation; continuing (maintaining an attitude) instant in prayer;

Praise God for what He is going to manifest in your life, even if you presently do not see it. Even though you are presently under pressure, be patient (Hebrews 6:12) and rejoice in hope of your coming deliverance. With every twist and turn in your Christian walk, stay open to the leading of the Holy Spirit through prayer.

II. Attitude Toward Other Believers (13–21)

12:13 distributing to the needs of the saints, given to hospitality.

Distributing (giving) to the necessity of saints; given to hospitality.

The true motive behind giving is to be a blessing, not to just receive a blessing. We give to help others and show them Jesus Christ, no to feed our ego.

12:14 ¶ Bless those who persecute you; bless and do not curse.

This is a command to act from your spirit and not from your flesh. Follow the word and not your emotions. This verse ties in with Matthew 5:10-12, Jesus' command to His disciples to do the same. Anyone who stands up for the Lord will face persecution from the world. We are not to return evil for evil. What you sow, you will eventually reap.

12:15 Rejoice with those who rejoice, and weep with those who weep.

This is a warning against resentment toward those who are blessed. Often, our reaction toward others who have received a blessing is, "Why not me? I have had a need for a longer time than they have. I have stood in faith longer, I should have received my answer first." The obvious response should be, "My turn is coming. If they received their answer, I might be next in line. God is no respecter of persons." It is also easy to look down on those who are crying or in pain and pass blame. "..they should have trusted God. Why don't they exercise patience?" Remember the times you have gone through problems and appreciated someone's encouragement, not their reprimands.

12:16 Be of the same mind toward one another. Do not set your mind on high things, but associate with the humble. Do not be wise in your own opinion.

Be of the same mind (think alike) one toward another. Mind not high things (stop thinking proud thoughts), but condescend (deflate yourself) to men of low estate (the humble and ordinary). Be not wise (arrogant) in your own conceits.

Let nothing be done through selfish ambition or conceit, but in lowliness of mind let each esteem others better than himself. Let each of you look out not only for his own interests, but also for the interests of others (Philippians 2:3,4).

This is the attitude Jesus took on Himself when He left heaven and joined us on earth to identify with our trials, griefs, weaknesses and temptations and left this as our example (see Philippians 2:5-8).

12:17 ❡ Repay no one evil for evil. Have regard for good things in the sight of all men.

Recompense (do not pay back) to anyone evil for evil. Provide things honest (think ahead) in the sight of all men (believer and unbeliever).

Paul is saying, do not stoop to the level of those who treat you with evil. React like Jesus did when He was reviled by Pilate. He did not react in evil, but left it in the hands of His Father (1 Peter 2:18-23). Vengeance does not belong to you, but to God (Romans 12:19).

12:18 If it is possible, as much as depends on you, live peaceably with all men.

There are times when it is not possible to live at peace with those who do wrong. The Bible condones aggression in times of war, crime or self-defense. Even those times are not times to react or act too quickly, but "as much as lies within you" to live at peace as long as possible. War should be a reaction, a defense, not something you initiate on others for no reason.

12:19 Beloved, do not avenge yourselves, but *rather* give place to wrath; for it is written, "Vengeance *is* Mine, I will repay," says the Lord.

Dearly beloved, avenge not yourselves (do not take revenge), but rather give place (defer) unto wrath: for it is written (in Deuteronomy 32:35), Vengeance (revenge) is mine; I will repay, says the Lord.

The Roman believers were judging each other and not letting God handle their wrath and anger. They were not casting their care on the Lord. You do not have the ability to repay. If someone does you dirty, don't pay them back, let God pay. You give them love and God will pay you back.

12:20 Therefore "If your enemy is hungry, feed him; If he is thirsty, give him a drink; For in so doing you will heap coals of fire on his head."

This is a quote from Proverbs 25:21, 22. If you have the ability at the time (v. 18 if it is possible) feed your enemy and give him drink. Heaping coals of fire on his head means you could cause conviction to come on him for how he has treated you. Returning good for evil can cause repentance to come to your enemy.

12:21 Do not be overcome by evil, but overcome evil with good.

Be not overcome (conquered) of (by) evil, but overcome (conquer) evil with good.

This verse is a summary of the last half of chapter 12.

13:1–14 Being Spiritual in the Natural

Christians live in a natural world as well as a spiritual world. The spiritual world gives wisdom and power to live in the natural.

Jesus said, we are to give to Caesar the things that belong to Caesar, as well as give to God the things that belong to God. These are two sides of the same coin.

I. Responsibility to Authority (1–7)

Just as there are laws that govern the spiritual world, there are laws that govern the natural. There are four divine institutions set up for the preservation of mankind in the natural world, free will, marriage, family and nationalism.

> **13:1 ¶ Let every soul be subject to the governing authorities. For there is no authority except from God, and the authorities that exist are appointed by God.**

Let every soul (every person in the human race) be subject (under the authority of) to the higher powers (*exousia*: authorities). For there is no power (authority) but of (from) God: the powers (authorities) that be (exist) are ordained of God.

Government was ordained by God, whether the government is just or becomes corrupt. If men have perverted government, they will answer to God. It is no different from the local church which was also ordained by God. If the pastor becomes corrupt, he will answer to God. The church is still the will and desire of God.

> **13:2 Therefore whoever resists the authority resists the ordinance of God, and those who resist will bring judgment on themselves.**

Whoever (believer or unbeliever) therefore that resists the authorities, resists the ordinance of God: and they that resist shall receive to themselves damnation (judgment).

This verse is addressed to lawbreakers, whether they are Christians or not. To resist the policeman, military, schoolteacher or boss has a judgment attached. This judgment can vary from fines, arrest, jail, prison and finally execution. God ordained the system of authority, whether the one executing the judgment is right or wrong. Your option is to accept the judgment or resist in a lawful manner. This is not damnation to hell, but judgment under God's system of law in the natural world. Laws and government help us control a world under Satan's rule.

13:3 For rulers are not a terror to good works, but to evil. Do you want to be unafraid of the authority? Do what is good, and you will have praise from the same.

For rulers (local, state and national leaders) are not a terror (threat) to good works (law abiding citizens), but to the evil (law breakers). Will you then not reverence the power (authorities)? do that which is good (lawful), and you shall have praise of (by) the same:

The same government that judges (v. 2) can praise (v. 3). It is up to you to obey God and His word and leaders set in this earth by Him.

13:4 For he is God's minister to you for good. But if you do evil, be afraid; for he does not bear the sword in vain; for he is God's minister, an avenger to *execute* wrath on him who practices evil.

For he (ruler) is the minister of God (in the natural order of government) to you for good (your own good). But if you do that which is evil, be afraid; for he bears not the sword (capital punishment) in vain: for he is the minister of God, a revenger to execute wrath upon him who does evil.

Capital punishment is the ultimate punishment for crime in the earth. In Paul's day the sentence was carried out by a man with a sword to cut off your head.

God is in favor of capital punishment and it is condoned in both the Old Testament (Genesis 9:6) and New.

Uses of the Word "Minister"

1. Pastor of a local church (Ephesians 3:7, 6:21, Colossians 1:23, 4:7)

2. Every believer (2 Corinthians 3:6, 4:1, 6:4)

3. Leaders of a nation (Romans 13:4)

13:5 Therefore *you* must be subject, not only because of wrath but also for conscience' sake.

Wherefore (as a result of vv. 1-4) you must needs be subject (under authority), not only for wrath (because you fear them), but also for conscience sake (you know it's right).

Now, Paul directs the subject to believers only. Just because you are born again and a citizen of heaven (Philippians 3:20), does not mean you do not obey the law. Quite the contrary, you should be a better citizen because you know the importance and biblical reasoning for human government. Verses 6 and 7 teach about paying taxes.

13:6 For because of this you also pay taxes, for they are God's ministers attending continually to this very thing.

For for this cause (government in authority) pay tribute (taxes) also (with unbelievers): for they are God's ministers, attending continually upon this very thing.

It is often a sore spot to pay taxes, especially when they seem higher than necessary. Christians are not exempt, but "you pay taxes also."

13:7 Render therefore to all their due: taxes to whom taxes *are due*, customs to whom customs, fear to whom fear, honor to whom honor.

Render (pay) therefore to all their dues (legitimate taxes): tribute (income taxes) to whom tribute is due; custom (indirect taxes) to whom custom; fear (respect) to whom fear; honor (praise) to whom honor.

"Render" is the same word Jesus used for paying taxes to Caesar. You are to pay whether it is a percentage of your earnings, custom, duties on foreign goods, local, county, state or national taxes. If God needs to send a fish with money in its mouth to pay your taxes, He will do it. He has done it before.

II. Responsibility to Neighbors (8–10)

Paul comments on our responsibility towards those with whom you work or know sociably.

13:8 ¶ Owe no one anything except to love one another, for he who loves another has fulfilled the law.

This is not a verse telling you it is God's command and will to be out of debt, take out a loan or mortgage or never charge any item. It is still in the context of service to your community, paying taxes and now paying your bills.

For the good of your relationship with others, keep your word. If you signed an agreement saying you would pay your electric bill, house payment, utilities or car payment on the fifteenth of the month, pay it and don't look for ways out of it. The only debt we can never pay off and will continue to owe, is our love debt to the world. Be an example of the character of God and operate in love toward all, especially in giving them the gospel. When you continue to love people, you fulfill the law (Galatians 5:14).

13:9 For the commandments, "You shall not commit adultery," "You shall not murder," "You shall not steal," "You shall not bear false witness," "You shall not covet," and if *there is* any other commandment, are *all* summed up in this saying, namely, "You shall love your neighbor as yourself."

For this, You shall not commit adultery, You shall not kill (murder), You shall not steal, You shall not bear false witness, You shall not covet; and if there be any other commandment, it is briefly comprehended in this saying, namely (in Leviticus 19:18), You shall love your neighbor as yourself.

When you walk in the flesh, you have a debt you owe to people. You cannot pay that debt from the flesh, you are controlled by sin, you are carnal. But, when you walk in the Spirit, you fulfill the law and owe no man anything, because you are keeping the law.

13:10 Love does no harm to a neighbor; therefore love *is* the fulfillment of the law.

Love works no ill to his neighbour: therefore love (*agape*) is the fulfilling of the law.

It is impossible to produce divine love when you are carnal, walking in the flesh. Divine love can only be produced from the Holy Spirit (Romans 5:5) in you as you walk in fellowship with the Lord.

III. Responsibility to the Gospel (11–14)

13:11 ¶ And *do* this, knowing the time, that now *it is* high time

to awake out of sleep; for now our salvation *is* nearer than when we *first* believed.

And that (walking in love), knowing the time (*kairos*: period of time, dispensation we live in), that now it is high time (*hora*: the hour) to awake out of sleep (carnality): for now is our salvation (ultimate salvation—The Rapture of the Church— see Romans 8:23) nearer than when we believed.

This is an urgent plea to walk in love, fulfill the law and get people born again because this dispensation of grace is rapidly coming to a close. Sleeping Christians is an analogy to carnality. Carnal Christians, out of fellowship and under the control of the flesh, are said to be "asleep (carnality) among dead people (sinners)" (Ephesians 5:8-15).

The prodigal was an example of this verse in Ephesians. He was saved but carnal, and living among the unbelievers and joining in their lifestyle until he came to himself (awoke) and rose up (arose) and went home (Christ gave him light).

We are commanded to be aware of the times we are living in and the shortness of time before Jesus returns for the Church. The time of our final redemption, the receiving of a resurrection body, is close at hand. Our dispensation is about to end.

13:12 The night is far spent, the day is at hand. Therefore let us cast off the works of darkness, and let us put on the armor of light.

The night is far spent (about to end), the day is at hand: let us therefore cast off the works of darkness, and let us put on the armour of light.

The Church Age is almost over. It is called "the night" because the world is still under Satan's control (2 Corinthians 4:4, Galatians 1:4, Ephesians 2:2). He is called the god and prince of this world's system. His rulership is almost over and will be terminated at the Battle of Armageddon.

Casting off the works of darkness begins with 1 John 1:9, repentance and confession of sins for the believer. Darkness is called works because they are the production of our life when we are under the control of the flesh which is still under the curse, the darkness of the world. The armor of light is the walk of the believer in fellowship with the Lord and under the control of the Holy Spirit in us. This is the same light Christ will give us when we return to fellowship with Him (Ephesians 5:14).

13:13 Let us walk properly, as in the day, not in revelry and drunkenness, not in lewdness and lust, not in strife and envy.

Let us walk (temporal life of sanctification) honestly (decently), as in the day; not in rioting (reveling, partying) and drunkenness (intoxication), not in chambering (illicit sex) and wantonness (lust, imaginations, inner adultery), not in strife (fight) and envying (inner jealousy toward others).

Walking is always an example of the Christian life after salvation, lived before men. When we are born again, we are said to be "seated" with Jesus. Walking is an example of sanctification, holiness or godliness before the world. It is the living out of the life inside of us. God can see what is in us. The world needs to see outwardly what God has done in our life.

13:14 But put on the Lord Jesus Christ, and make no provision for the flesh, to *fulfill its* lusts.

But put on the Lord Jesus Christ, and make not provision (forethought) for the flesh, to fulfil the lusts of it.

Once you return to fellowship, give thought to the future of how not to fall back into the same trap again. You have control over the flesh and should have from this time on. Study of the word and walking in fellowship with God through the Holy Spirit is our assurance we will not fall back into carnality. "If you abide in me (remain in fellowship), and my word abides in you (study of the word), ask what you will and it shall be done.

14:1–23 Weak and Strong Believers

This chapter addresses the problem of the weak and carnal believer who lives the Christian life by works.

I. The Weak Believer (1)

14:1 ❡ Receive one who is weak in the faith, *but* not to disputes over doubtful things.

Him that (He who) is weak in the faith receive, but not to doubtful disputations (arguments).

This is not a new believer, but one whose whole criteria for Christianity is legalism (spirituality based on human good works). We are to receive that person into the church and our fellowship, but not to argue or straighten him out.

II. Characteristics of the Weak Believer

A. Guilty
He has a guilt complex. Somewhere in his past he has failed and is trying to make up for it with many good works. He also feels bad when he is rejected by others.

B. Apathetic
He is not interested in the word. He is more interested in experiences over scripture.

C. Judgmental
He is quick to judge others who do not observe his own ideas of holy days, eating and dress codes.

D. Manipulative
He is constantly trying to fit others into his mold and is a spiritual bully.

E. Nosy
He tends to get into everyone's business. He has no respect for the privacy of others. He always has an opinion to give you about your conduct, and he is a trouble maker in the congregation. He usually hides this behind a facade of "lets pray for so and so." He tries to make himself look good by discrediting others.

III. Grace Believer versus Legalistic Believer (2–14)

A. Food

14:2 For one believes he may eat all things, but he who is weak eats *only* vegetables.

For one believes that he may eat all things: another, who is weak, eats herbs (vegetables).

The grace believer is one who believes he may eat all things. He is filled with the word and his beliefs are based on scripture. The weak believer eats vegetables. He is a believer who thinks eating meat is wrong because it involved killing life of some kind. After all the Bible says somewhere, "thou shalt not kill." So, if you eat vegetables you are more spiritual than those carnal believers who eat meat.

Food is natural, never spiritual. Food laws under Moses were never spiritual but designed to teach of Jesus Christ. People did not get sick because they ate pork, shrimp or any other forbidden meats. The only time, Old Testament or New, that food interferes into spiritual areas is in overeating. Diet and exercise do not produce health. Health comes from God and obedience to His word and will (Proverbs 3:8, 4:22, 16:24, Jeremiah 33:6, 3 John 2). Diet and exercise produce fitness. You can be fit and not healthy. You can also be healthy and not fit.

14:3 Let not him who eats despise him who does not eat, and let not him who does not eat judge him who eats; for God has received him.

As a grace believer, do not judge or look down your nose at the legalist. You are now worse off than they are (Matthew 7:1-5). Do not judge other believers by your standards.

14:4 Who are you to judge another's servant? To his own master he stands or falls. Indeed, he will be made to stand, for God is able to make him stand.

Proverbs 30:10 says we all belong to the Lord, so let God handle the person if you do not like what they are doing. One believer, or a group of believers, do not determine the status of other believers. The master (God) determines the status for each servant.

B. Observance of Days

14:5 ¶ One person esteems *one* day above another; another esteems every day *alike*. Let each be fully convinced in his own mind.

One man (legalistic believer) esteems one day above another: another (grace believer) esteems every day alike. Let every man be fully persuaded in his own mind.

The strong, grace believer sees no difference between days. "If it is sin on Sunday, it has to be a sin on Monday. It really does not matter what day we worship, God is the same each day. Christmas day is a great celebration, but we should celebrate Jesus' birth every day. Easter is not a one day event, but our source of power all year." He lives each day as unto the Lord and doesn't do more on one day than another.

The legalistic believer sees evil behind days and celebrations and wants everyone to think like he does. He celebrates when he convinces someone else to give up Christmas trees, Easter eggs, or Sunday worship for Saturday instead.

We are to be fully persuaded in our own mind. We are to love each other despite our differences. Love is higher than petty differences. Let the Holy Spirit and the word of God convince the legalistic, immature believer. We become fully persuaded by the word (Romans 4:21, 8:38).

C. Neither Should Judge

Verse 6 tells us to mind our own business whether we regard days, food or not.

14:6 He who observes the day, observes *it* to the Lord; and he who does not observe the day, to the Lord he does not observe *it*. He who eats, eats to the Lord, for he gives God thanks; and he who does not eat, to the Lord he does not eat, and gives God thanks.

He (weak believer) who regards the day, regards it unto the Lord; and he (strong believer) who regards not the day, to the Lord he does not regard it. He (strong believer) who eats, eats to the Lord, for he gives God thanks; and he (weak believer) who eats not, to the Lord he eats not, and gives God thanks.

If you make an issue over keeping certain days, do it to the Lord, don't push your doctrines off on others. If you do not observe days, don't condemn others who do. You do it to the Lord only. Whether you eat meat or vegetables only, don't argue with each other. Eat the meat and give God thanks. We only stand accountable to the Lord, not each other or even ourselves. Our criteria is the word.

14:7 For none of us lives to himself, and no one dies to himself.

For none of us lives to himself (to his own advantage), and no man dies to himself.

Whether you live or die we should glorify God. Never push to promote yourself or your own way of seeing things.
Verse 8 amplifies verse 7.

14:8 For if we live, we live to the Lord; and if we die, we die to the Lord. Therefore, whether we live or die, we are the Lord's.

For whether (if) we live, we live unto the Lord; and whether we die, we die unto the Lord: whether we live therefore, or die, we are the Lord's (give God glory).

We are the Lord's possession. Since we belong to Him, we should give Him glory. Get rid of your self-righteous hypocritical attitude. If you are convicted or not over food, days, etc, then just keep it between you and God.

14:9 For to this end Christ died and rose and lived again, that He might be Lord of both the dead and the living.

Jesus had to die to become Lord. Now that He is Lord, don't set your own standards, go by His. If we live by His standards, we need to die to our own. In verses 10 through 12, Jesus will do all judging. We are not to judge each other, we are infringing on His job. We can only judge ourselves.

14:10 But why do you judge your brother? Or why do you show contempt for your brother? For we shall all stand before the judgment seat of Christ.

But why do you judge your brother? or why do you set at nought (despise, look down on) your brother? for we shall all (spiritual, carnal, grace, legalistic) stand before the judgment seat of Christ.

"We shall" is future tense but it is definite. It is yet to come (after the Rapture) but there is no escape. The Judgment Seat of Christ is mentioned in other verses (1 Corinthians 3:11-16, 2 Corinthians 5:10, 2 Timothy 2:12, 13, Hebrews 6:7-12).

D. Points on Morality

1. Christianity is not morality. Morality is a by-product of Christianity.

2. Morality has no dynamics. The Christian way of life is supernatural and must be executed through the power of the Holy Spirit. Morality alone is usually promoted by self-righteousness or religion. Jesus condemned this in Matthew 23 in the lives of the Pharisees.

3. Morality is essential to the functioning of all mankind, Christian or sinner. If you try to be born again or spiritual by being moral it makes you no different than a sinner.

4. Sources of morality.

   a. The Holy Spirit (Romans 8:2-4, Titus 2:11,12). This is divine good.

   b. The flesh (Isaiah 64:6, Titus 3:5). This is human good.

14:11 For it is written: "As I live, says the Lord, every knee shall bow to Me, and every tongue shall confess to God."

For it is written (in Isaiah 45:23), As I live, says the Lord, every knee shall bow to me, and every tongue shall confess to God.

Homage goes to Jesus and confession of His Lordship goes to the Father. The believer will be at the Judgment Seat of Christ because he bowed at the new birth.
The unbeliever will be at the Great White Throne Judgment because he never bowed. All people on the earth, in heaven and in hell will bow at the Second Advent.

14:12 ⁋ So then each of us shall give account of himself to God.

So then (application) every one of us (believers) shall give account of himself to God.

This account will be given at the Judgment Seat of Christ.

14:13 Therefore let us not judge one another anymore, but

rather resolve this, not to put a stumbling block or a cause to fall in our brother's way.

By doing so we have taken the Lord's job and we are incapable of handling it. So, do not judge others, judge yourself. Check your intentions and motives at all times.

E. Four Laws of the Christian Life

1. The Law of Liberty: This is toward the Lord. We are free to do as we please before God.

2. The Law of Love: This is toward believers. When we are around other Christians, we must refrain from doing certain things which could offend them.

3. The Law of Expediency: This is toward sinners. We refrain from doing certain things because we do not want to put a stumbling block in front of them to keep them from accepting Jesus.

4. The Law of Sacrifice: Toward ourselves to accomplish greater things for God. Paul stayed single, some became eunuchs, and Paul made tents for a short time, etc.

14:14 ¶ I know and am convinced by the Lord Jesus that *there is* nothing unclean of itself; but to him who considers anything to be unclean, to him *it is* unclean.

I know (knowledge of the word), and am persuaded (confident) by the Lord Jesus, that there is nothing unclean of (in) itself: but to him (legalistic believers) who esteems (reckons—see Romans 6:11) anything to be unclean, to him it is unclean.

The word gives us confidence and stability toward the convictions of men (2 Corinthians 5:1-8). To the person an issue is unclean, not to God or the grace believer. The legalistic believer is not our enemy, but his attitude is. Seeing the difference is the most important issue to the grace believer.

IV. The Strong Believer (15–23)

Verse 15 is teaching of the mature believer's attitude toward the legalistic weak believer.

14:15 Yet if your brother is grieved because of *your* food, you are no longer walking in love. Do not destroy with your food

the one for whom Christ died.

The legalistic weak brother is grieved by your liberty. If your brother is offended at your liberty, do not fail to walk in love. The law of love looks at people through the eyes of the Lord. Jesus was free but he refrained from certain things not to offend and cause people shipwreck. One of the greatest manifestations of love is to refrain from activity to keep from hindering another Christian.

14:16 Therefore do not let your good be spoken of as evil;

Let not then your good (liberty) be evil spoken of (criticized by weak believers):

It is better to not eat or drink anything which would offend. It is over by the time the meal is over. If you are an offense, the criticism will last for quite awhile.

14:17 for the kingdom of God is not eating and drinking, but righteousness and peace and joy in the Holy Spirit.

For the kingdom of God (all believers, the Church) is not food and drink; but righteousness, and peace, and joy in the Holy Spirit.

The kingdom of God is not a physical kingdom, but spiritual. Therefore food and drink are not part of God's kingdom. We live in a spiritual kingdom energized by the Holy Spirit. Meat will not produce joy nor stop it. The Holy Spirit brings joy and your carnality stops it.

14:18 For he who serves Christ in these things *is* acceptable to God and approved by men.

For he who in these things (meat and drink) serves Christ (does all things as unto the Lord) is acceptable to God, and approved by men.

If you will be led by the Spirit in all things you will do good in both worlds, spiritual and natural.

14:19 ⸿ Therefore let us pursue the things *which make* for peace and the things by which one may edify another.

Let us (believers who are strong) therefore follow (pursue) after the things which make for (produce) peace, and things wherewith (by which) one may edify (build up) another.

14:20 Do not destroy the work of God for the sake of food. All things indeed *are* pure, but *it is evil* for the man who eats with offense.

For food does not destroy the work of God. All things (food and drink) indeed are pure; but it is evil for that man (legalist) who eats with offence (condemnation, guilt).

Food will not destroy righteousness, peace or joy. The things in the natural world will never destroy the spiritual.

14:21 *It is* good neither to eat meat nor drink wine nor *do anything* by which your brother stumbles or is offended or is made weak.

It is good neither to eat flesh, nor to drink wine, nor anything whereby (by which) your brother (weak one) stumbles, or is offended, or is made weak.

Wine drinking is mentioned here with eating certain types of food. Wine drinking was a controversial issue in that day as it is ours.
Verses 22 and 23 are the conclusion of the chapter.

14:22 Do you have faith? Have *it* to yourself before God. Happy is he who does not condemn himself in what he approves.

Do you have faith? have (keep) it to yourself before God. Happy is he that condemns not himself in that thing which he allows (permits).

Are you persuaded you are right? Show your maturity and mind your own business. You can do whatever you want if you are not convicted over it and don't intentionally cause anyone else to stumble. Your standard should be the word and your reward should be a life pleasing to God.

14:23 But he who doubts is condemned if he eats, because *he does* not *eat* from faith; for whatever *is* not from faith is sin.

And he (legalist) who doubts is damned (condemned) if he eat, because he eats not in faith: for whatever is not of faith (known from the word) is sin (to you).

If someone has been taught that a certain food or drink is wrong, he feels condemned if he takes it because he is doubting and confused. He should not eat because someone else does, but because the word has freed him. He can then eat and drink free from guilt.

15:1–23 Being Mature in Christ

I. Responsibilities (1–14)

Romans 15 talks about the responsibilities of the mature believer.

15:1 ¶ We then who are strong ought to bear with the scruples of the weak, and not to please ourselves.

We then that are strong (*dunamis*) ought to bear the infirmities (weaknesses) of the weak (immature believer—see ch. 14), and not to please ourselves (only use the law of liberty).

This is further amplified in Galatians 6:2, telling the strong to help bear the burdens and aid in the recovery of the weak and carnal believer.

15:2 Let each of us please *his* neighbor for *his* good, leading to edification.

Let every one of us (as strong believers) please his neighbour for his good to edification.

There are things you have to do even when you do not want to so your weak brothers and sisters can grow. You should never impose your convictions on them and cause them to stumble.

15:3 For even Christ did not please Himself; but as it is written, "The reproaches of those who reproached You fell on Me."

For even Christ pleased not himself; but, as it is written, (Psalm 69:9) The reproaches (sins) of them who reproached you (God the Father) fell on me.

Jesus took the sins of all unbelievers and weak believers on Himself when He died on the cross. This is our example to care more for the stumbling and immature Christian than we do ourselves. His death on the cross was to forgive sins, so sinners could become saints, and weak believers could grow up to be strong.

A. How Maturity Is Developed

15:4 For whatever things were written before were written for our learning, that we through the patience and comfort of the Scriptures might have hope.

For whatever things were written beforetime (Old Testament scriptures) were written for our learning, that we (in the Church Age) through patience and comfort (security) of the scriptures might have hope (confidence).

Old Testament scriptures are important to us in the Church Age. Knowledge of the entire word of God is important. Almost every verse quoted and fulfilled in the New Testament came from the Old. The Old Testament strongly teaches patience in the life of faith. Also many comforting scriptures in the Old Testament bring confidence today.
In verse 5, we see that likemindedness comes from knowledge of the word.

15:5 Now may the God of patience and comfort grant you to be like-minded toward one another, according to Christ Jesus,

Now the God (the source) of patience and consolation (comfort) grant you to be likeminded one toward another according to (the standard of) Christ,

One of Paul's wishes for us is to have comfort in the Christian life. Comfort is a result of patience. Once we enter into the life of faith and rest, we begin to think like Jesus Christ did in His earthly life. We then know the word, apply it to life and exercise the mind of Christ.

15:6 that you may with one mind *and* one mouth glorify the God and Father of our Lord Jesus Christ.

That you may (it's up to you) with one mind and one mouth glorify God, even the Father of our Lord Jesus Christ.

The word in our heart causes us to first think like Jesus Christ, then to speak and act like Him. Our thoughts glorify God as well as our actions.

15:7 ¶ Therefore receive one another, just as Christ also received us, to the glory of God.

Wherefore (as a result) receive one another (spiritual, carnal, weak or strong), as Christ also received us to the glory of God.

Jesus received us when we were sinners, lost, etc. And He loved us too much to leave us that way. Our love toward each other gives God glory.

B. Maturity and the Old Testament
Verses 8 through 12 teach the mature believer is oriented to the Old Testament ministry of Christ.

> **15:8 Now I say that Jesus Christ has become a servant to the circumcision for the truth of God, to confirm the promises *made* to the fathers,**

Now I say that Jesus Christ was (became) a minister of the circumcision (Jew) for the truth of God, to confirm (ratify) the promises made to the fathers (Abraham, Isaac, Jacob and other O.T. prophets):

Verse 8 is the Old Testament dealings to the Jews. Verses 9 through 12 is to the Gentiles.

> **15:9 and that the Gentiles might glorify God for *His* mercy, as it is written: "For this reason I will confess to You among the Gentiles, And sing to Your name."**

And that the Gentiles might (it was up to them) glorify God for his mercy (grace); as it is written (Psalm 18:49), For this cause I will confess to (of) you among the Gentiles, and sing to your name.

This tells the Old Testament assignment to the Jewish nation, to take the gospel and word to the Gentile nations. David, the one who wrote this verse, fulfilled it by witnessing to the Gentiles. Many of his court, singers, musicians and military were believers through David's witness by mouth, written word and lifestyle. They operated in patience, praise and worship to God, giving God glory through the life of Gentiles as well as Jews.

> **15:10 And again he says: "Rejoice, O Gentiles, with His people!"**

And again he says (Deuteronomy 32:43), Rejoice, you Gentiles, with his people (Jews).

Deuteronomy was written by Moses to the Jews under the law. Even during the law, the message from the Jewish nation was salvation through faith in the Lord and living by the word. The message was never salvation or spirituality by the law.

15:11 And again: "Praise the Lord, all you Gentiles! Laud Him, all you peoples!"

And again (Psalm 117:1), Praise the Lord, all you Gentiles; and laud (applaud, extol) him, all you people.

David saw great praise coming from the Gentiles toward the God of Israel. They sang praises to God side by side with the Jews in David's choir and with the saints in the tabernacle.

15:12 And again, Isaiah says: "There shall be a root of Jesse; and He who shall rise to reign over the Gentiles, in Him the Gentiles shall hope."

And again, Isaiah says (in Isaiah 11:10), There shall be a root of Jesse, and he that shall rise to reign over the Gentiles; in him shall the Gentiles trust.

Isaiah not only prophesied that Jesus would save the Gentiles as well as the Jews, he saw it come to pass in his own day. Isaiah was a great evangelist to the Gentiles. During the time of great rejection of Israel toward God and a future of exile in Babylon, the Gentiles accepted Jehovah in great numbers through the ministry of Isaiah and were shocked that the Jews were worshipping Baal, the god they had just rejected for the true Lord. Isaiah not only saw conversions, but great praise and worship coming from the Gentiles as David did.

Paul has been saying in verses 8 through 12 that the mature believer in the Church Age understands God's dealings with Gentiles as well as Jews throughout Old and New Testament history.

15:13 ¶ Now may the God of hope fill you with all joy and peace in believing, that you may abound in hope by the power of the Holy Spirit.

Now the God of hope (confidence) fill you with all joy and peace in believing (through your faith), that you may abound in hope, through the power of the Holy Spirit.

Joy and peace should always accompany our faith. This comes from maintaining fellowship with God through forgiveness of our daily sins (1 John 1:4,9). There is no true joy in carnality. In fellowship you are empowered by the Holy Spirit. Out of fellowship you are empowered by the flesh.

15:14 ¶ Now I myself am confident concerning you, my brethren, that you also are full of goodness, filled with all knowledge, able also to admonish one another.

And I myself also am persuaded of you, my brethren, that you also (along with me) are full of goodness, filled with all knowledge, able also to admonish one another.

You cannot admonish without knowledge. Counsel to others demands knowing the word of God.

II. Paul's Example (15–33)

Verse 15 teaches of the ministry of Paul and degrees of authority.

15:15 Nevertheless, brethren, I have written more boldly to you on *some* points, as reminding you, because of the grace given to me by God,

Nevertheless, brethren, I have written the more boldly to you in some sort (part), as putting you in mind, because of the grace that is given to me of God,

In verse 14, we were told we can admonish one another. But there are offices in the body of Christ given to teach and instruct us in areas we cannot get on our own. We need the offices of apostle, prophet, evangelist and pastor and teacher (1 Corinthians 12:28, Ephesians 4:7-11). We have studied the offices given to the congregation (Romans 12:3-8), but Paul's office carries more authority. He speaks through that office now, the apostle. He calls it a grace here and in Romans 12:3. His office carries more authority than that of a congregation grace of a teacher or exhorter. This grace of Paul's, as with us, is given to us by God and the Lord Jesus Christ (Galatians 1:1, Ephesians 1:1,2). He has spoken to the Romans more boldly than they would have spoken to each other. Paul's boldness is never given in anger, but in love though it may seem harsh. It is always to build up the saints by putting them back on the right track.

Verse 16 teaches of the responsibility of the minister.

15:16 that I might be a minister of Jesus Christ to the Gentiles, ministering the gospel of God, that the offering of the Gentiles might be acceptable, sanctified by the Holy Spirit.

That I should be the minister (*diakonos*: server) of Jesus Christ to the Gentiles, ministering the gospel of God, that the offering up of the Gentiles might be (become) acceptable, being sanctified by the Holy Ghost.

Paul is a servant of Jesus Christ to the Gentiles. The only thing a minister gives is the gospel and the word of God (Acts 6:4).
The "offering up of the Gentiles" is worship and praise to God for the message Paul has given to them. Only worship given in line with the word is acceptable to God. This brings a tremendous obligation on the minister to bring people to a point of acceptability to God. Praise acceptable to God also brings on the anointing of the Holy Spirit Who sanctifies our worship. The Holy Spirit agrees with the word.

A. Paul Boasts in Grace

15:17 Therefore I have reason to glory in Christ Jesus in the things *which pertain* to God.

I have therefore whereof (a reason) I may glory through Jesus Christ in those things which pertain to God.

It is best only to boast in the things which God has done through you. Then the glory goes to the Lord.

15:18 For I will not dare to speak of any of those things which Christ has not accomplished through me, in word and deed, to make the Gentiles obedient—

For I will not dare to speak of any of those things which Christ has not wrought by (worked through) me, to make the Gentiles obedient (to the gospel), by word (preaching) and deed (demonstrations of the Holy Spirit),

Paul will not speak of the things he has personally done, only that which God has accomplished through his ministry. The heathen (the Gentiles) have been won to Jesus by Paul's preaching and by supernatural demonstrations of the Holy Spirit. Both are given to win the lost (Mark 16:15-18). Both are given to us by God, the gospel we preach and the gospel we demonstrate.

15:19 in mighty signs and wonders, by the power of the Spirit of God, so that from Jerusalem and round about to Illyricum I have fully preached the gospel of Christ.

Through mighty signs and wonders, by the power of the Spirit of God; so that from (starting from) Jerusalem, and round about unto Illyricum (modern Yugoslavia), I have fully preached the gospel of Christ.

The gospel has not been fully preached until signs and wonders accompany the preaching of the gospel (Mark 16:20).

15:20 And so I have made it my aim to preach the gospel, not where Christ was named, lest I should build on another man's foundation,

There is a striving to keep the supernatural as part of the message of salvation. There are so many pressures to back off speaking with tongues, healing and miracles and the revelation gifts of the Holy Spirit. Those who only speak the message of salvation are only partially preaching the gospel.
Paul also went to places where the gospel had never been preached. This again is a reference to Gentiles (Rome, Galatia, Philippi, Thessalonica, Berea, Ephesus).

15:21 but as it is written:"To whom He was not announced, they shall see; and those who have not heard shall understand."

But as it is written (in Isaiah 52:15), To whom he was not spoken of (preached to), they shall see: and they that have not heard shall understand.

Paul used the message and signs and wonders to win over the Gentiles. This could not have been done in his own power and his own wisdom.

B. Paul's Traveling Plans
In these verses Paul tells of his plans to visit Jerusalem and return to Rome.

15:22 ¶ For this reason I also have been much hindered from coming to you.

For which cause (preaching the gospel to the Gentiles) also I have been much hindered from coming to you.

Paul has had a great desire to return to Rome for some time, but his preaching has kept him busy and away.

15:23 But now no longer having a place in these parts, and having a great desire these many years to come to you,

Paul has evangelized in every place the Lord has instructed him to and there is no more places to preach. He is now free to return and visit Rome.

15:24 whenever I journey to Spain, I shall come to you. For I hope to see you on my journey, and to be helped on my way there by you, if first I may enjoy your *company* for a while.

Whenever I take my journey into Spain, I will come to you: for I trust to see you on my journey, and to be brought on my way thitherward (there) by (to) you, if first I be somewhat filled (with enjoyment) with your company.

Verses 25 through 28 is Paul's present plans to visit Jerusalem.

15:25 But now I am going to Jerusalem to minister to the saints.

This ministry is not preaching, but delivering money (2 Corinthians 9:1).

15:26 For it pleased those from Macedonia and Achaia to make a certain contribution for the poor among the saints who are in Jerusalem.

For it has pleased those of Macedonia and Achaia to make a certain (financial) contribution for the poor saints who are at Jerusalem.

15:27 It pleased them indeed, and they are their debtors. For if the Gentiles have been partakers of their spiritual things, their duty is also to minister to them in material things.

It has pleased them verily (truly); and their debtors they are. For if the Gentiles have been made partakers of their spiritual things, their duty is also to minister unto them in carnal (natural) things.

It is the obligation and responsibility of those who hear the gospel from those called into the ministry, to give of their finances to cause the gospel and the word to continue to be preached and demonstrated. This responsibility is not out of pressure or necessity, but love toward God and those who bring us the word of eternal life and daily victory.

15:28 Therefore, when I have performed this and have sealed to them this fruit, I shall go by way of you to Spain.

When therefore I have performed this, and have sealed to them this fruit (offering), I will come by you (going) into Spain.

15:29 But I know that when I come to you, I shall come in the fullness of the blessing of the gospel of Christ.

Paul has a few things to complete before visiting Rome and the saints there. Once he does them, he will come in the fullness of what God has for them. His mind will have nothing else to think about. He will be fully prepared to give them all God has given him.

15:30 ¶ Now I beg you, brethren, through the Lord Jesus Christ, and through the love of the Spirit, that you strive together with me in prayers to God for me,

Now I beseech (command) you, brothers, for (through) the Lord Jesus Christ's sake, and for the love of the Spirit, that you strive together with me in your prayers to God for me;

Paul wants the Romans to pray for him for the ministry sake, to further the gospel in the power of the Holy Spirit. There is a striving, working, in prayer. The flesh does not like or want the discipline. This is not striving between each other, but with yourself, your own flesh.

15:31 that I may be delivered from those in Judea who do not believe, and that my service for Jerusalem may be acceptable to the saints,

That I may be delivered from them that do not believe in Judaea; and that my service (financial offering) which I have for Jerusalem may be accepted (acceptable) by the saints;

Paul is under some of the greatest pressure of his ministry from the legalistic believers in Jerusalem. He has been successful in facing them before, but now it is different. The opposition will no longer debate with Paul in front of the church leadership and have resorted to looking for ways to just kill Paul. His life is in danger by simply going to Jerusalem.

15:32 that I may come to you with joy by the will of God, and may be refreshed together with you.

His desire after going to Jerusalem was to go to Rome and be refreshed by seeing the saints there again.

15:33 Now the God of peace *be* with you all. Amen.

Now (as for now) the God of peace be with you all. Amen.

16:1–21 Final Words

I. Roman's Hall of Fame (1–16)

Most of Romans 16 is the hall of fame for the Church at Rome.

16:1 ¶ I commend to you Phoebe our sister, who is a servant of the church in Cenchrea,

I commend to you Phebe our sister (in the Lord), who is a servant (*dia-konos*: server) of the church which is at Cenchrea:

Phoebe is the woman who carried this letter from Corinth to Rome. She is considered to be a female deacon, a deaconess in the church at Cenchrea, an eastern seaport of Corinth.

16:2 that you may receive her in the Lord in a manner worthy of the saints, and assist her in whatever business she has need of you; for indeed she has been a helper of many and of myself also.

Paul is saying, "don't look down on her because she is a woman, but receive her as a deaconess, as any minister in the service of the Lord." Phebe has operated in the helps ministry to many ministers, including Paul himself.
Verses 3 through 5 teach of Aquila and Pricilla.

16:3 Greet Priscilla and Aquila, my fellow workers in Christ Jesus,

Priscilla was a housewife, Aquila a businessman. Both had effective ministries. Priscilla stood in faith with her husband. They met in Rome and were married. They later moved to Ephesus and there met Paul and were born again (1 Corinthians 16:19). They later moved back to their home city of Rome and established a church there (Romans 16:5). While they lived in Ephesus they met Apollos. Apollos was eloquent but ignorant of the word of God. Priscilla and Aquila taught him the word and he went on to be a great minister (Acts 18:24-28).

16:4 who risked their own necks for my life, to whom not only

I give thanks, but also all the churches of the Gentiles.

Sometime in the past, they saved Paul's life. Not only they, but members of the church had also helped spare Paul through direct intervention and prayer.

16:5 Likewise *greet* the church that is in their house. ¶ Greet my beloved Epaenetus, who is the firstfruits of Achaia to Christ.

A church is not a building but the people who meet in the building. Paul so plainly said this calling the people who met in the house, the church. Aquila and Priscilla had one of three local churches in Rome. Paul now begins to mention some of the believers who attended and worked in those churches. Epaenetus was one of Paul's first converts in Greece (Achaia).

16:6 Greet Mary, who labored much for us.

There is a great mention of women in this passage. Paul knew women deaconesses, eldresses, and others who ministered to the needs of the church and Paul himself.

16:7 Greet Andronicus and Junia, my countrymen and my fellow prisoners, who are of note among the apostles, who also were in Christ before me.

Salute Andronicus and Junia, my kinsmen (probably cousins), and my fellowprisoners, who are of note (well known) among the apostles, who also were in Christ before me.

Andronicus and Junia were related to Paul and were born again before him. They gained a reputation among the church leadership and even had their faith put to the test by imprisonment for being Christians.

16:8 ¶ Greet Amplias, my beloved in the Lord.

Amplias and the next nine disciples are only mentioned here in Romans.

16:9 Greet Urbanus, our fellow worker in Christ, and Stachys, my beloved.

Salute (greet) Urbane, our helper (fellow worker) in Christ, and Stachys my beloved.

These were workers with Paul, some known and others friends, well loved.

16:10 ¶ Greet Apelles, approved in Christ. Greet those who are of the *household* of Aristobulus.

Aristobulus was Herod's son that he finally killed when he became old and senile.

16:11 Greet Herodion, my countryman. Greet those who are of the *household* of Narcissus who are in the Lord.

Salute (greet) Herodion my kinsman (another kinsman). Greet those who are of the household of Narcissus, who are in the Lord.

History tells us Narcissus was an early martyr.

16:12 ¶Greet Tryphena and Tryphosa, who have labored in the Lord. Greet the beloved Persis, who labored much in the Lord.

These three are all women who worked with Paul and put in much labor for the Lord's work, or more labor than most others.

16:13 Greet Rufus, chosen in the Lord, and his mother and mine.

Rufus had a brother, Alexander. His father was Simon of Cyrene who carried Jesus' cross (Mark 15:21).
Verse 14 is probably the second Roman church and verse 15 the third.

16:14 Greet Asyncritus, Phlegon, Hermas, Patrobas, Hermes, and the brethren who are with them.

Hermas is a woman and Hermes a man. Again, part of a group who were helpers alongside Paul.

16:15 Greet Philologus and Julia, Nereus and his sister, and Olympas, and all the saints who are with them.

More disciples who put the work of the ministry and their love for Paul above themselves.

16:16 ¶ Greet one another with a holy kiss. The churches of

Christ greet you.

Salute (greet) one another with an holy kiss. The churches of Christ (in Corinth) salute (greet) you.

Kissing on the cheek in the ancient world was considered a greeting between good friends and especially between close disciples of the Lord.

II. Avoid Division (17–20)

16:17 ¶ Now I urge you, brethren, note those who cause divisions and offenses, contrary to the doctrine which you learned, and avoid them.

Now I beseech (command) you, brothers, mark (tag with a sign and stay away) them who cause divisions and offences contrary to the doctrine (word) which you have learned; and avoid them.

This is a command to avoid those Christians whose criteria in life is anything but the word. We are commanded in the word to avoid worldliness (not the people in the world) and unstable believers who cause division (Proverbs 6:19, 2 Thessalonians 3:14,15).

16:18 For those who are such do not serve our Lord Jesus Christ, but their own belly, and by smooth words and flattering speech deceive the hearts of the simple.

For they who are such serve not our Lord Jesus Christ, but their own belly; and by good words and fair speeches (flattery) deceive the hearts of the simple (immature).

They may be saved, but they do not serve the Lord Jesus. They serve their own belly (*choilia*), emotions or sensual appetites. These believers know how to appeal and sway the emotions of the immature believers. They are a danger to the local church and the stability of those who attend. Good church leadership knows when to cut ties with them and show them the door.
In verse 19, Paul commends their obedience to the word of God.

16:19 For your obedience has become known to all. Therefore I am glad on your behalf; but I want you to be wise in what is

good, and simple concerning evil.

For your obedience is come abroad (become known) to all men. I am glad therefore on your behalf: but yet I would have you wise unto (in) that which is good, and simple concerning evil.

Paul does not want the believers in Rome to be mixed up, not truly knowing what is good and evil (Hebrews 5:14). When the believer knows the word, good and evil are easy to recognize and distinguish.

16:20 And the God of peace will crush Satan under your feet shortly. ⁋ The grace of our Lord Jesus Christ *be* with you. Amen.

And the God of peace will bruise (crush) Satan under your feet shortly. The grace of our Lord Jesus Christ be with you. Amen.

This is a reference to the ultimate victory over Satan, the Second Advent. Satan was defeated by the Lord Jesus at the resurrection, but Satan's ultimate banishment from the earth will occur at the end of the Tribulation when Jesus returns to set up His kingdom. Satan will no longer be the god of this world, Jesus will.

III. Paul's Companions (21–24)

16:21 ⁋ Timothy, my fellow worker, and Lucius, Jason, and Sosipater, my countrymen, greet you.

Lucius was a prophet and teacher mentioned in Acts 13:1. He has known Paul since the time of his ministry separation with Barnabas. Jason protected Paul's life and was dragged before the judge but released in Acts 17:5-9. Sosipater was another relative of Paul's.

16:22 ⁋ I, Tertius, who wrote *this* epistle, greet you in the Lord.

Tertius was a scribe who took Paul's dictation or notes and wrote this epistle.

16:23 ⁋ Gaius, my host and *the host* of the whole church, greets you. Erastus, the treasurer of the city, greets you, and Quartus, a brother.

Paul was staying in the home of Gaius (1 Corinthians 1:14), a minister in

Corinth. Erastus was the treasurer in Corinth. He traveled with Timothy on Paul's orders (Acts 19:22).

16:24 The grace of our Lord Jesus Christ *be* with you all. Amen.

IV. The Mystery (25-27)

16:25 ¶ Now to Him who is able to establish you according to my gospel and the preaching of Jesus Christ, according to the revelation of the mystery kept secret since the world began

Now to him who is able to establish (stabilize) you according to my gospel, and the preaching of Jesus Christ, according to the revelation of the mystery, which was kept secret since the world began,

Once we become a Christian, only God's word will stabilize us in life (Isaiah 33:6). And a certain part of the New Testament (the epistles of Paul, Peter, John, etc.) are best equipped to stabilize us because they are specifically designed for our dispensation, the Church Age. This is the mystery, kept secret since the beginning of the ages and revealed now to us (Ephesians 3:1-11, Colossians 1:25,26).

16:26 but now made manifest, and by the prophetic Scriptures made known to all nations, according to the commandment of the everlasting God, for obedience to the faith—

But now (Church Age) is made manifest, and by the scriptures of the (New Testament church) prophets, according to the commandment of the everlasting God, made known to all nations for the obedience of faith:

There can be no true obedience to God's commands today without an understanding of the New Testament epistles and an understanding of the time period we live in.

16:27 to God, alone wise, *be* glory through Jesus Christ forever. Amen.

God's glory comes to us through Jesus Christ.

Reference Book List

Barclay, William, 1976. *New Testament Words*. Westminster: John Knox Press.

Jamison, Robert; Brown, David & Fausset, A.R., 1997. *A Commentary on the Old and New Testaments* (3 Volume Set). Peabody, MA: Hendrickson Publishers.

Strong, James H., 1980, 15th Edition. *Strong's Exhaustive Concordance of the Bible*. Nashville, TN: Abingdon Press.

Strong, James & Thayer, Joseph, 1995. *Thayers Greek-English Lexicon of the New Testament: Coded with Strong's Concordance Numbers*. Peabody, MA: Hendrickson Publishers.

Unger, Merrill, 1996. *Vine's Complete Expository Dictionary of Old and New Testament Words: With Topical Index*. Nashville, TN: Thomas Nelson.

Vincent, Marvin R., 1985, *Vincent Word Studies in the New Testament* (4 Volume Set). Peabody, MA: Hendrickson Publishers.

Wuest, Kenneth, 1980, Second Edition. *Word Studies from the Greek New Testament* (4 Volume Set). Grand Rapids: MI: William B. Eerdmans Publishing Company.

Zodhiates, Spiros, 1991. *The Complete Word Study New Testatment* (Word Study Series). Chatanooga, TN: AMG Publishers.

The writings of Arthur W. Pink.

The writings and audio recordings of Donald Grey Barnhouse.

Meet Bob Yandian

From 1980 to 2013, Bob Yandian was the pastor of Grace Church in his hometown of Tulsa, Oklahoma. After 33 years, he left the church to his son, Robb, with a strong and vibrant congregation. During those years, he raised up and sent out hundreds of ministers to churches and missions organizations in the United States and around the world. He has authored over thirty books and established a worldwide ministry to pastors and ministers.

He is widely acknowledged as one of the most knowledgeable Bible teachers of this generation. His practical insight and wisdom into the Word of God has helped countless people around the world to live successfully in every area of the daily Christian life.

Bob attended Southwestern College and is also a graduate of Trinity Bible College. He has served as both instructor and Dean of Instructors at Rhema Bible Training Center in Broken Arrow, Oklahoma.

Bob has traveled extensively throughout the United States and internationally, taking his powerful and easy to apply teachings that bring stability and hope to hungry hearts everywhere. He is called "a pastor to pastors."

Bob and his wife, Loretta, have been married for over forty years, are parents of two married children, and have five grandchildren. Bob and Loretta Yandian reside in Tulsa, Oklahoma.

Contact Bob Yandian Ministries

Email: bym@bobyandian.com

Phone:

(918) 250-2207

Mailing Address:

Bob Yandian Ministries

PO Box 55236

Tulsa, OK 74155

www.bobyandian.com

Other Books by Bob Yandian

Calling and Separation
Decently and in Order
Faith's Destination
From Just Enough to Overflowing
God's Word to Pastors
How Deep Are the Stripes?
Leadership Secrets of David the King
Morning Moments
One Flesh
Proverbs
Spirit Controlled Life
The Bible and National Defense
Understanding End Times
Unlimited Partnership
What If the Best Is Yet to Come?
When God is Silent
A New Testament Commentary Series (sold individually or as a set):

> *Acts l*
> *Acts ll*
> *Colossians*
> *Ephesians*
> *Galatians*
> *James*
> *Philippians*
> *Romans*

PRAYER OF SALVATION

God loves you—no matter who you are, no matter what your past. God loves you so much that He gave His one and only begotten Son for you. The Bible tells us that "...whoever believes in Him shall not perish but have eternal life" (John 3:16 NIV). Jesus laid down His life and rose again so that we could spend eternity with Him in heaven and experience His absolute best on earth. If you would like to receive Jesus into your life, say the following prayer out loud and mean it from your heart.

Heavenly Father, I come to You admitting that I am a sinner. Right now, I choose to turn away from sin, and I ask You to cleanse me of all unrighteousness. I believe that Your Son, Jesus, died on the cross to take away my sins. I also believe that He rose again from the dead so that I might be forgiven of my sins and made righteous through faith in Him. I call upon the name of Jesus Christ to be the Savior and Lord of my life. Jesus, I choose to follow You and ask that You fill me with the power of the Holy Spirit. I declare that right now I am a child of God. I am free from sin and full of the righteousness of God. I am saved in Jesus' name. Amen.

If you prayed this prayer to receive Jesus Christ as your Savior for the first time, please contact us on the Web at **www.harrisonhouse.com** to receive a free book.

Or you may write to us at
Harrison House • P.O. Box 35035 • Tulsa, Oklahoma 74153